John R. Sweney

Joyful Sound

A Collection of New Hymns and Music, with Familiar Selections

John R. Sweney

Joyful Sound
A Collection of New Hymns and Music, with Familiar Selections

ISBN/EAN: 9783337089894

Printed in Europe, USA, Canada, Australia, Japan

Cover: Foto ©Thomas Meinert / pixelio.de

More available books at **www.hansebooks.com**

THE JOYFUL SOUND

A COLLECTION OF

NEW HYMNS AND MUSIC,
WITH FAMILIAR SELECTIONS.

EDITORS:

JNO. R. SWENEY AND WM. J. KIRKPATRICK.

"Salvation! O the Joyful Sound!
What pleasure to our ears!
A sovereign balm for every wound,
A cordial for our fears."

PHILADELPHIA:

Published by JOHN J. HOOD, 1013 Arch St.

Copyright, 1889, by John J. Hood.

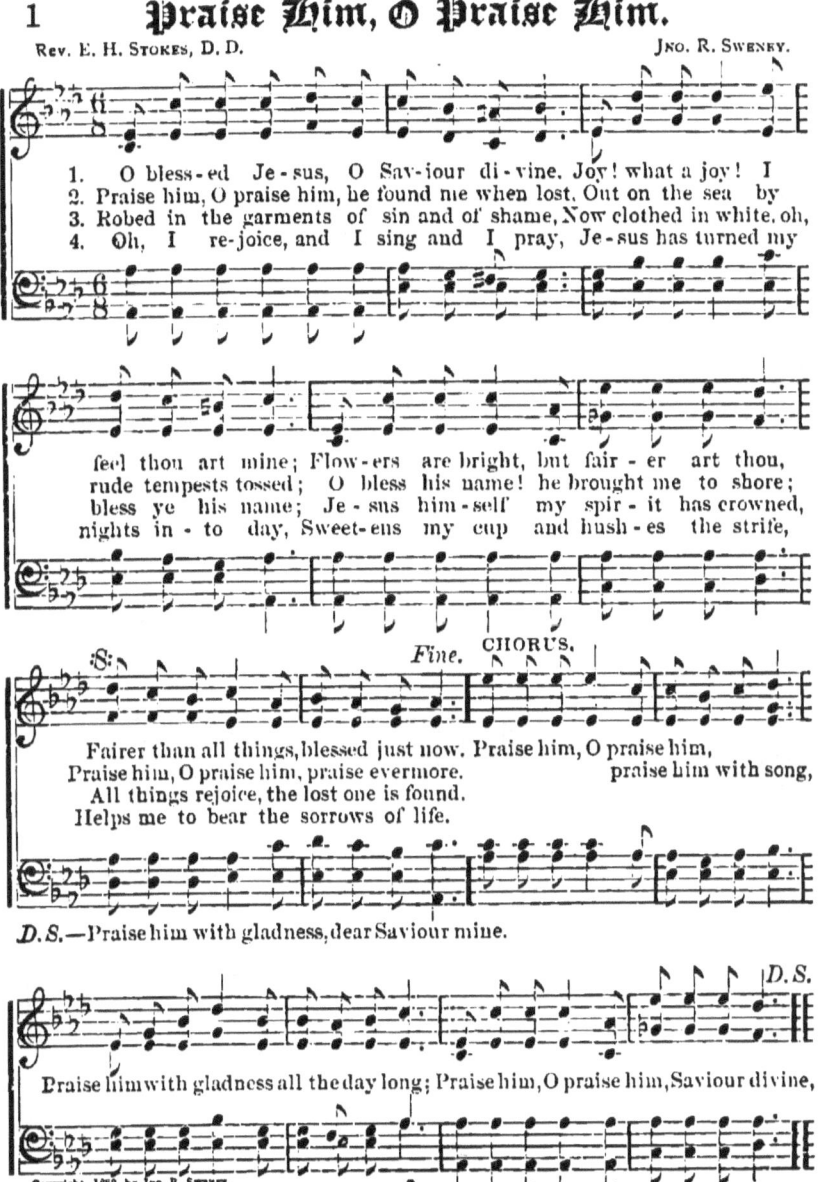

I Will Praise the Lord To-Day.

E. A. BARNES.   "With my song will I praise him."—Ps. xxviii. 7.   WM. J. KIRKPATRICK.

1. I will praise the Lord to-day, For the Lord is good to me: And his
2. I will praise the Lord to-day, For his name is more than sweet: And I
3. I will praise the Lord to-day, For his word is life and love: And the
4. I will praise the Lord to-day, For the Lord has ransomed me; He has

love ap- pears as the sweetest gift, 'Mid the blessings that I see.
gath- er strength for the toils of life As I worship at his feet.
hope he gives is a bless - ed hope, For it lifts my soul a - bove.
set his seal on this soul of mine, That his glo- ry I may see.

CHORUS.

Therefore my heart greatly rejoic- eth, Therefore my heart greatly rejoiceth,

Therefore my heart greatly rejoic - eth, And with my song will I praise him.

Copyright, 1889, by Wm. J. Kirkpatrick.

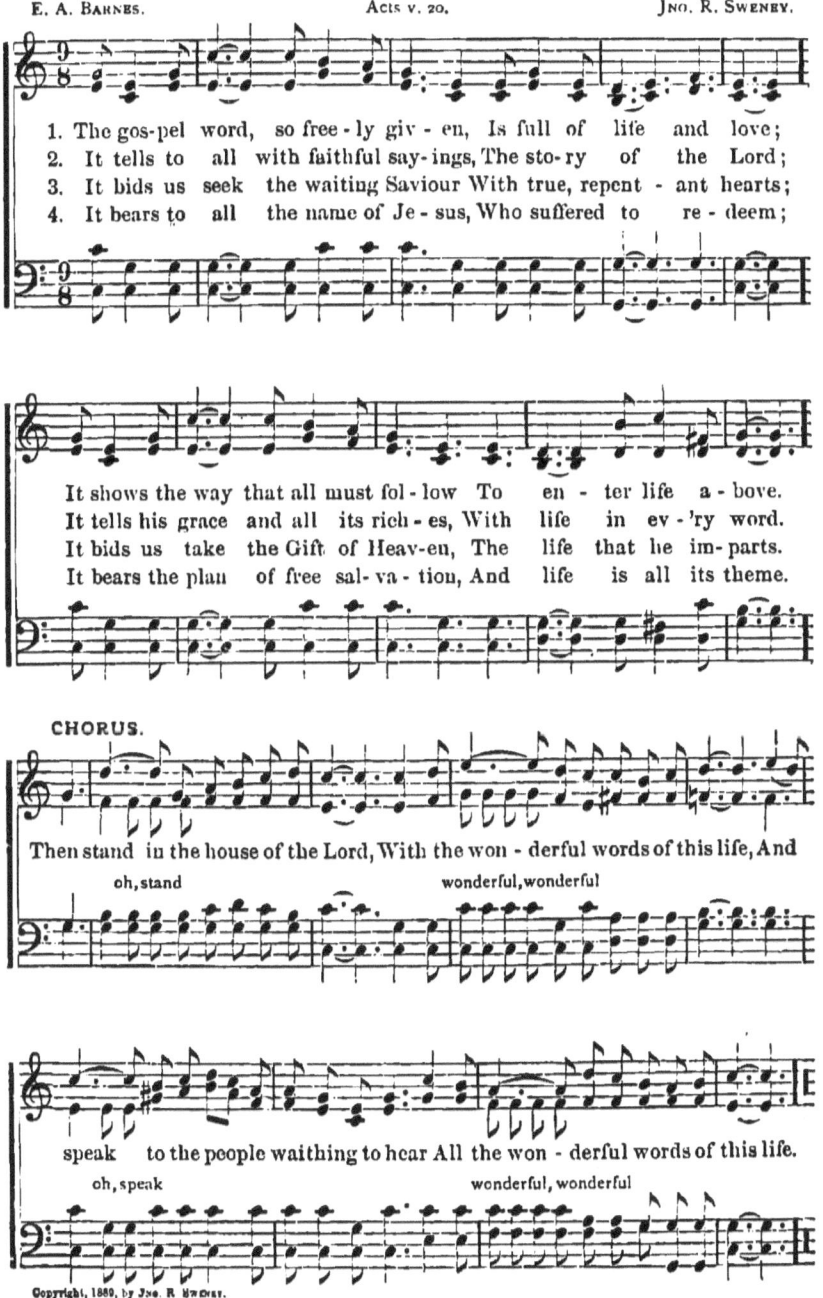

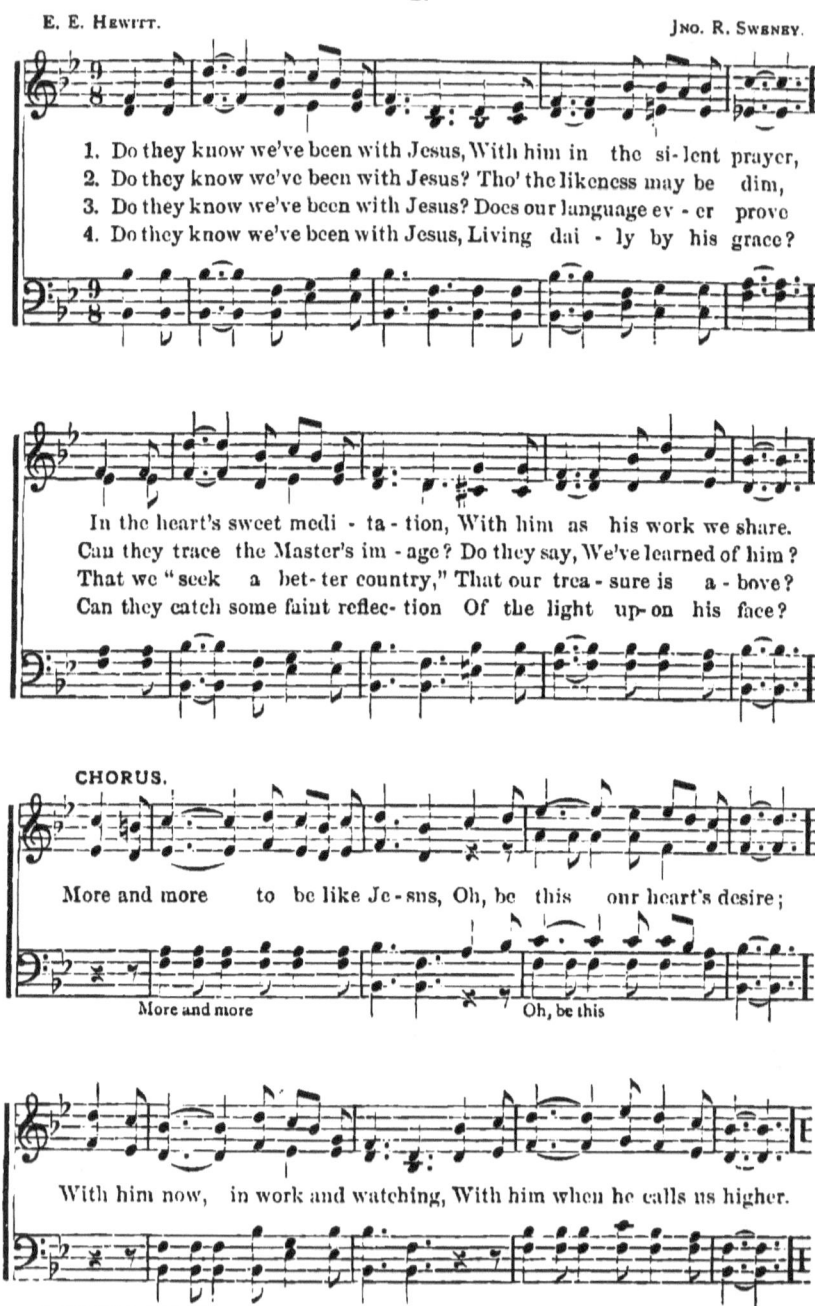

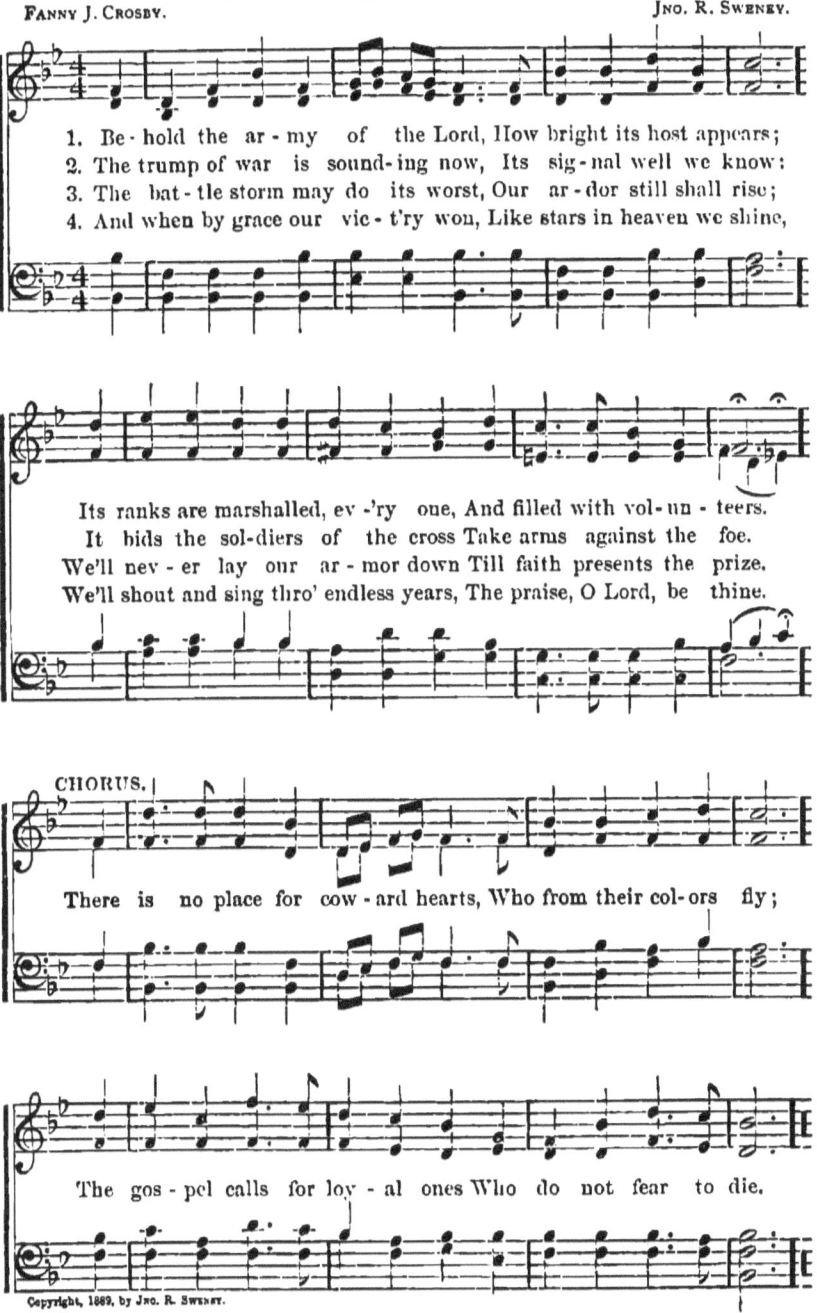

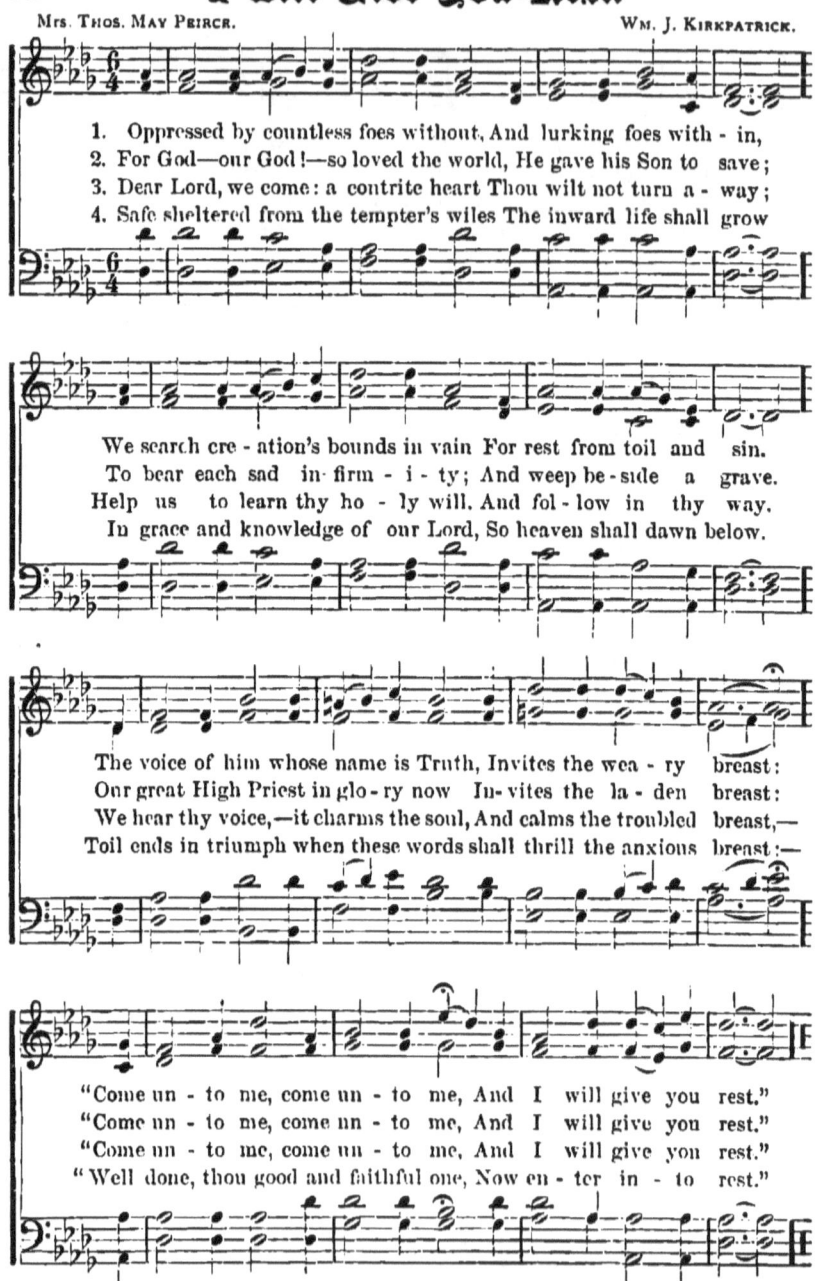

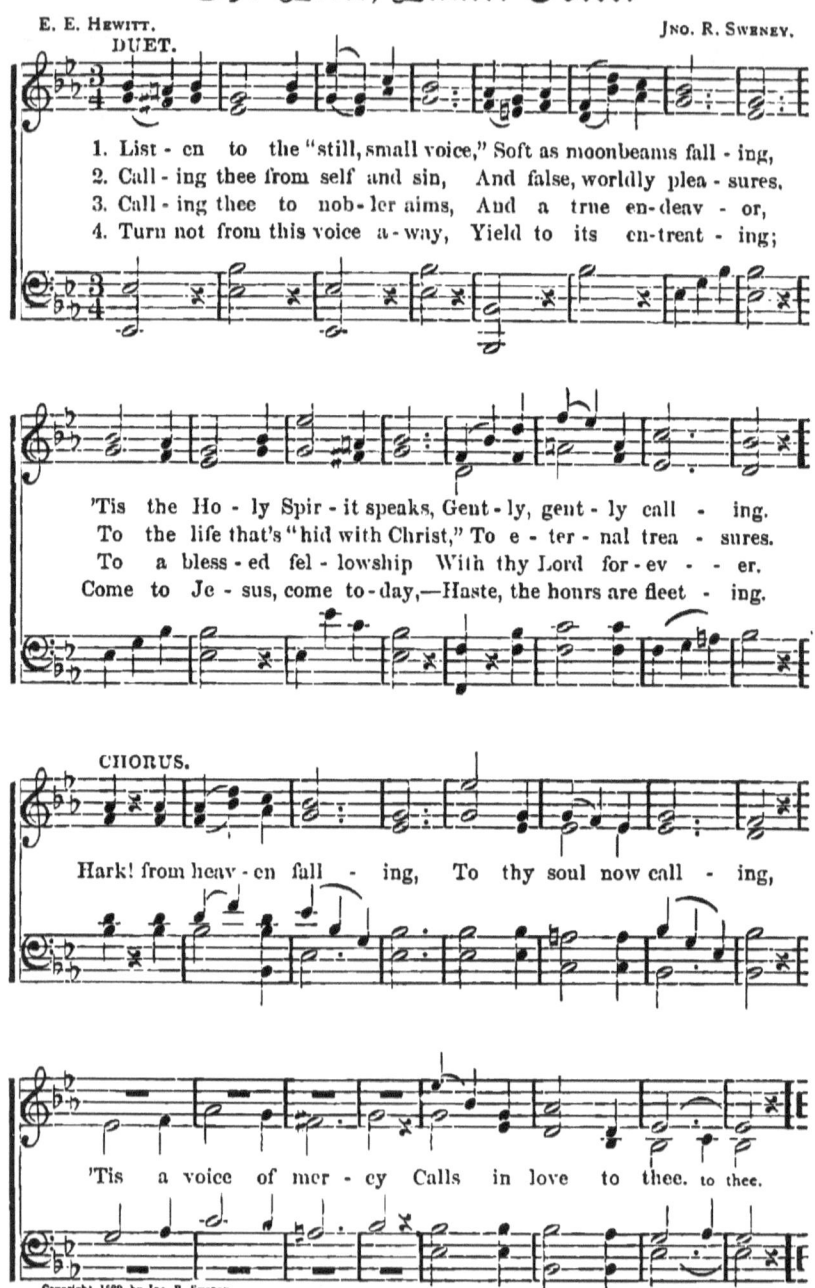

18. Best of All.

Rev. C. W. Ray, D. D.
Wm. J. Kirkpatrick.
Andante.

1. Jesus all my grief is sharing, He my mansion is preparing, When I'm trembling and despair-ing, He will ev-er hear my call; When the storms around me sweeping, Tho' in helplessness I'm sleeping, I am safe in his own keep-ing, This to me is best of all: Best of all, best of all, I am safe in his own keeping, This to me is best of all.

2. Jesus loves and watches o'er me, When astray he will restore me; Angel guards he sends before me, Lest in fa-tal snares I fall; With his friends he hath enrolled me, By his might he will uphold me, In his arms he will en-fold me, This to me is best of all: Best of all, best of all, In his arms he will enfold me, This to me is best of all.

3. Jesus loves and he will guide me, All I need he will provide me, In his bo-som he will hide me, When the woes of life ap-pal; He will hear my feeblest sighing, Needful grace to me supply-ing, He'll be with me when I'm dy-ing, This to me is best of all: Best of all, best of all, He'll be with me when I'm dying, This to me is best of all.

Copyright, 1889, by Wm. J. Kirkpatrick.

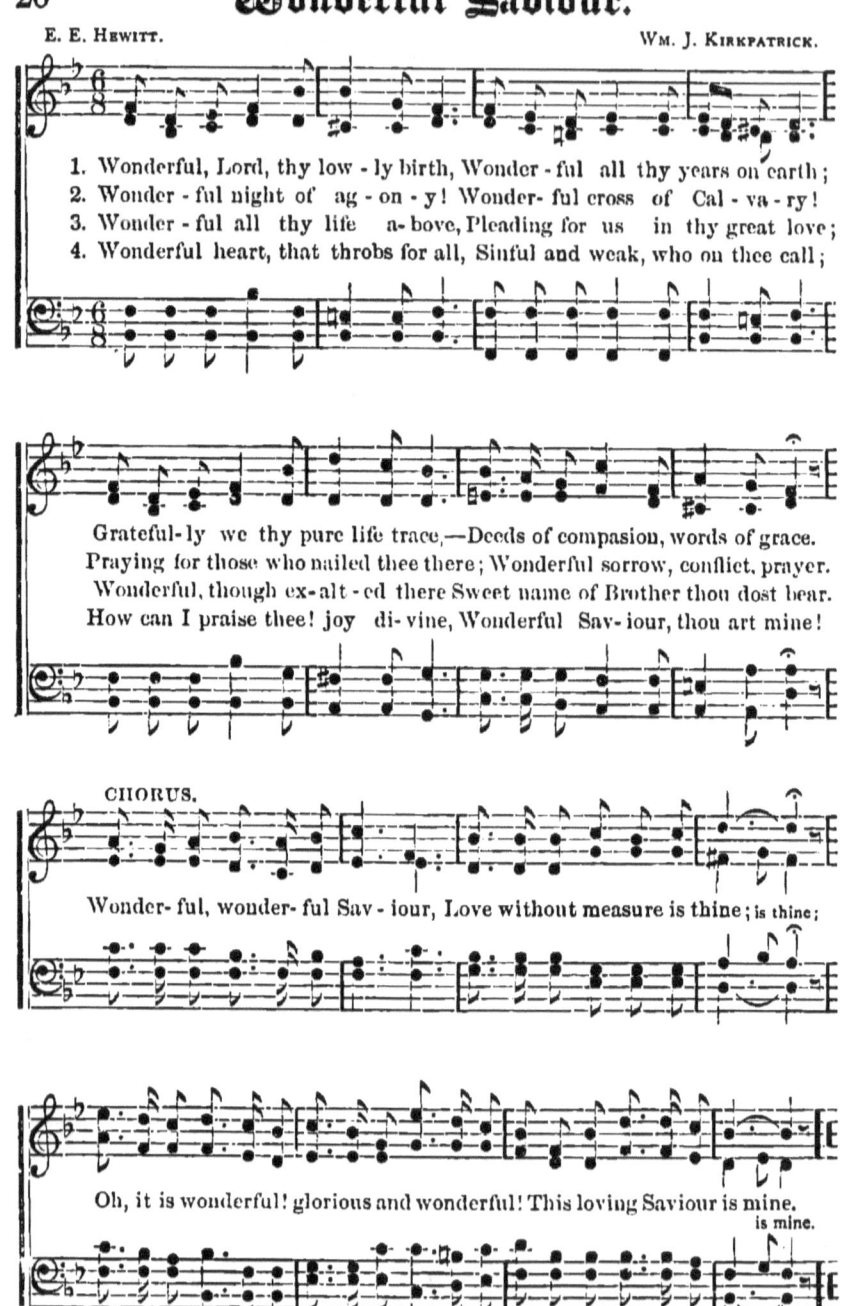

Let Me Into Nothing Fall. 21

THE topic for the Young People's Meeting at Ocean Grove, July 10th, 1887, was "The Friend of Sinners." A young man spoke upon the topic, saying, "Let me into nothing fall; Jesus is my all in all."

M. W. MORSE. JNO R. SWENEY.

1. Whene'er I think of Jesus, The sinner's Friend indeed, Who at heaven's court is stand-ing For ev - en me to plead; When I think he died to save me, When wandering in sin, How in softest tones he called me To come and fol- low him. Oh, let me in - to nothing fall,—Jesus is my all in all; Yes, let me in - to nothing fall,—Jesus is my all in all.

2. Whene'er I think of Je-sus, And his great love to me, My soul can't keep from sing-ing,— His foll'wer I would be; His grace to me has promised To help me on my way, As on thro' life I journey And press to endless day.

3. Whene'er I think of Je-sus, Oh, wondrous thought to me! With him I'll live for-ev - er, His glo-ry I may see; Then I'll sing of his great good-ness, His name will I a-dore; I am so glad he saves me Just now and ev - er - more.

Copyright, 1889, by Jno. R. Sweney.

5 I am trusting thee for power,
These can never fail;
Words that thou thyself shalt give me
Must prevail.

6 I am trusting thee, Lord Jesus;
Never let me fall;
I am trusting thee for ever,
And for all.

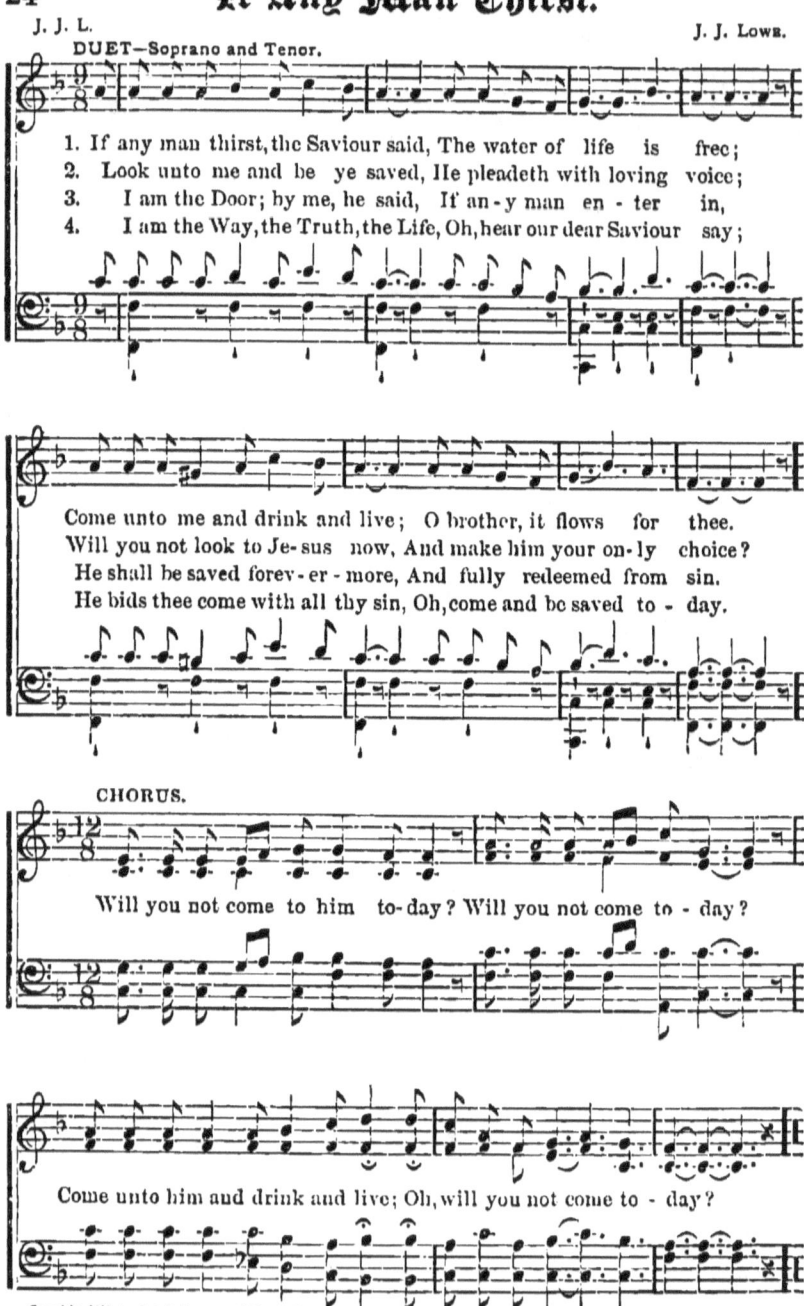

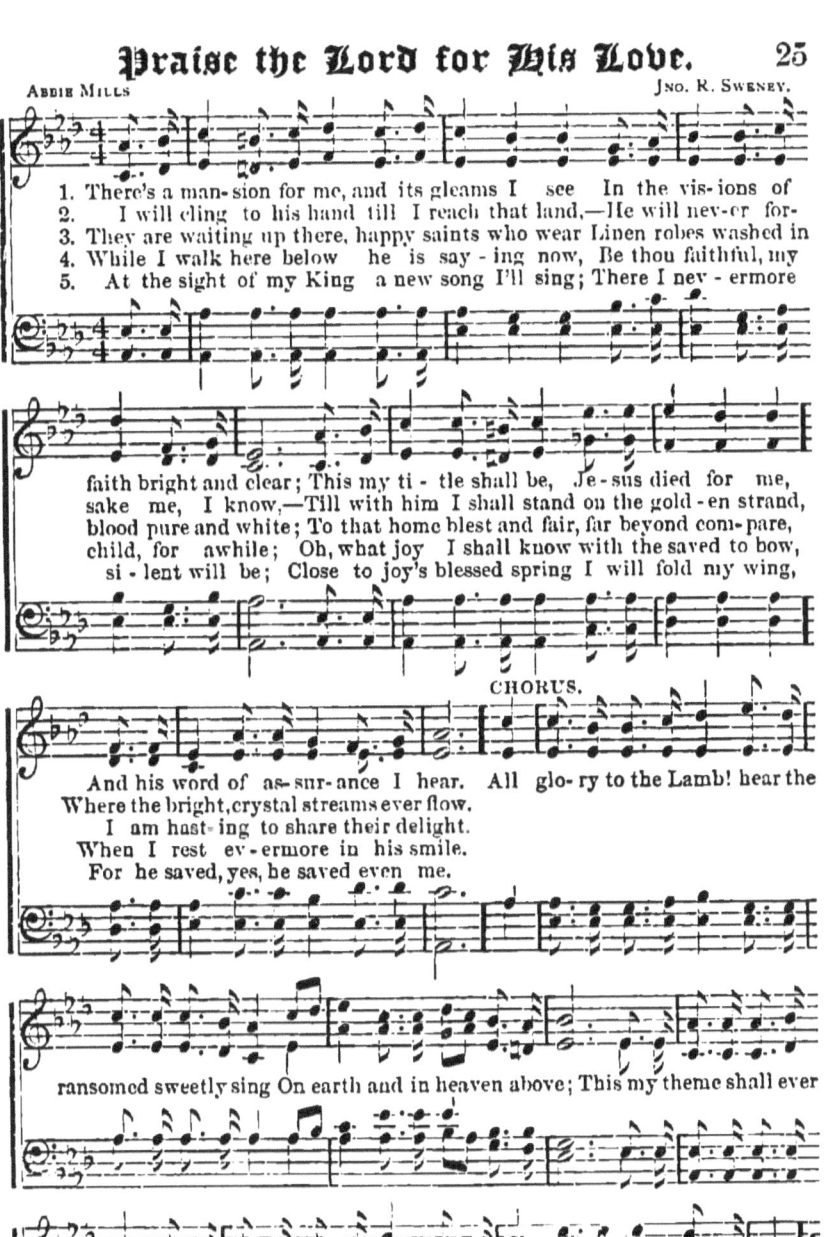

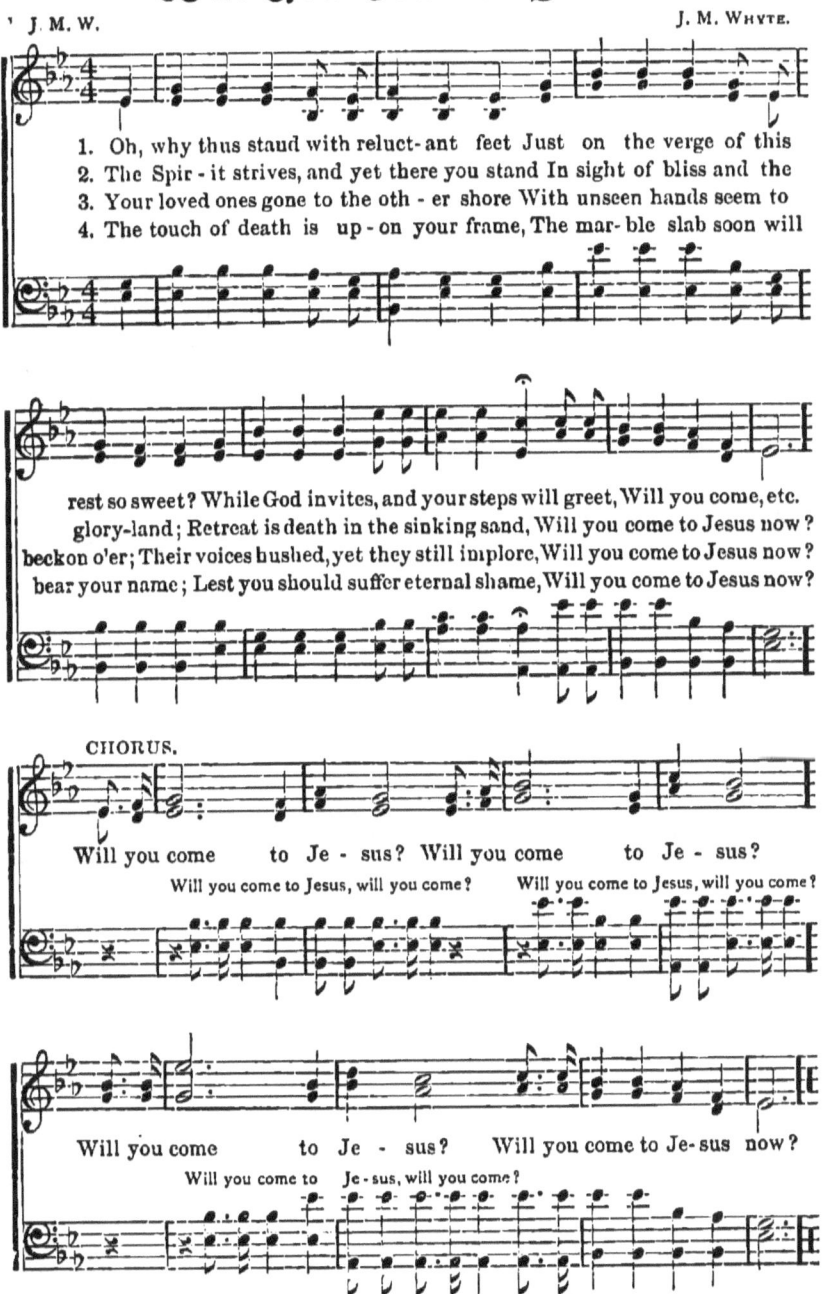

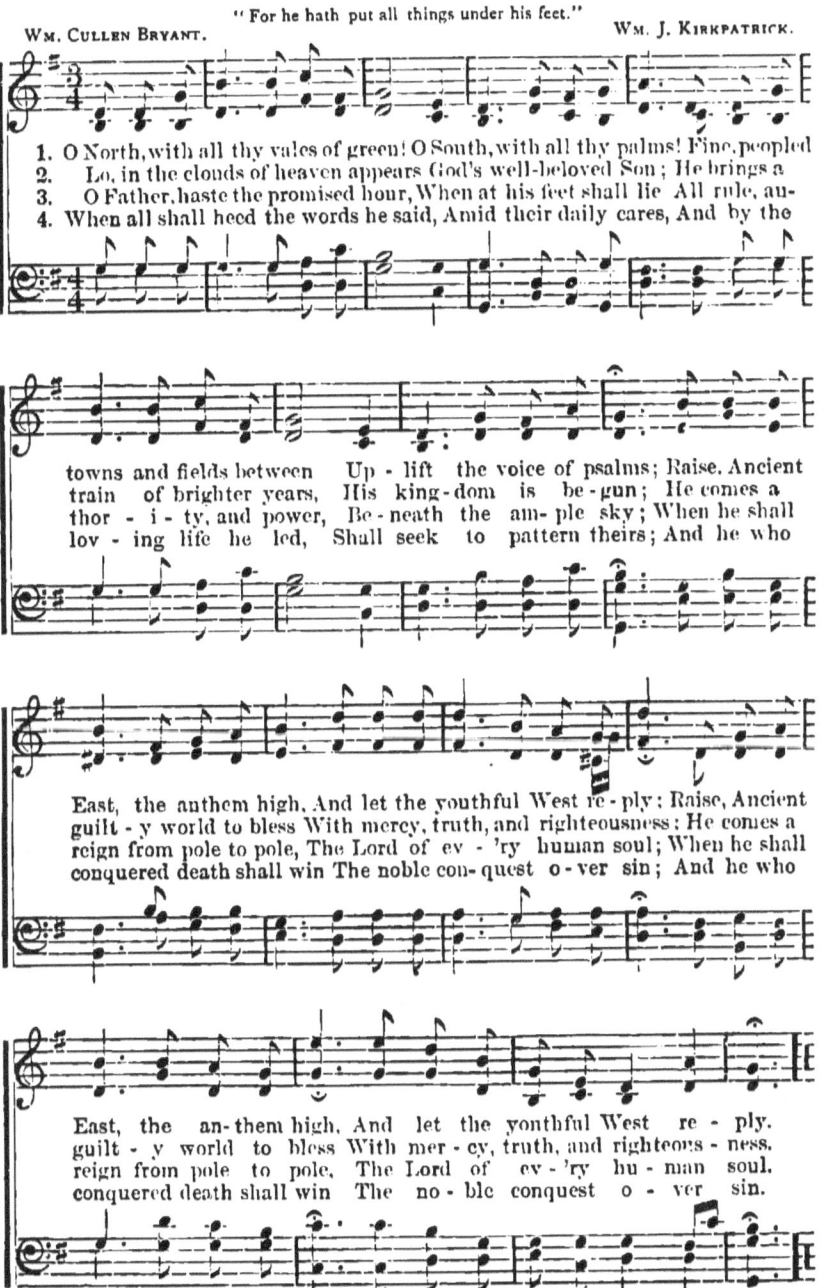

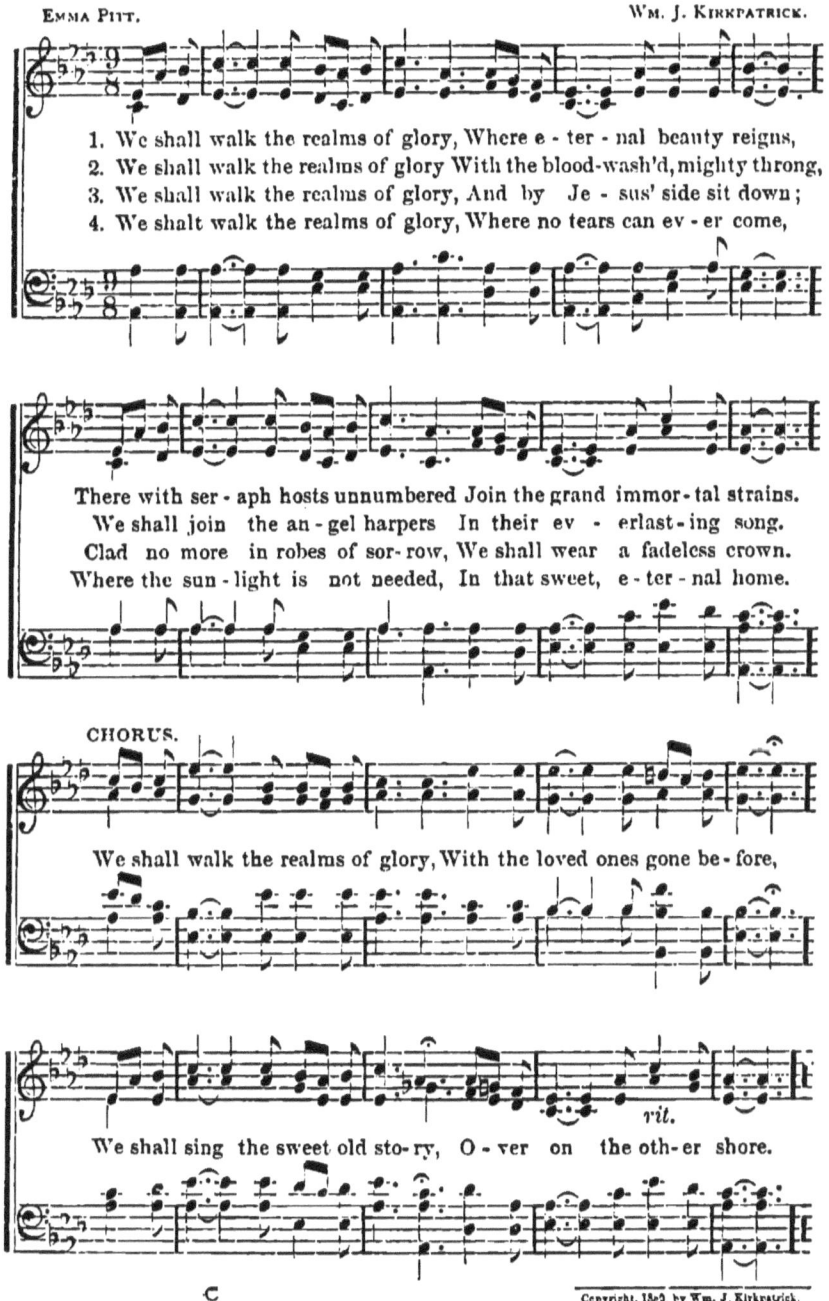

Take the Hand.

FANNY J. CROSBY.   WM. J. KIRKPATRICK.

1. Take the hand thy Saviour gives thee, Hold it fast within thine own;
2. Take the love that ne'er deceives thee, Love that makes thee all its own,
3. Take the peace none else can give thee, Hide it deep within thy breast;
4. Take thy all - suffi - cient Saviour, Thou wilt find no friend so dear;

It will lead thee to the riv - er That pro - ceed - eth from his throne.
Take it free - ly, like the wa - ters From the riv - er near the throne.
Like the riv - er clear as crys - tal It will soothe thy care to rest.
He will crown thee at the riv - er, On - ly be thou faithful here.

CHORUS.

Riv - er of Life . . . that spark - les free, . . . Riv - er of
Riv - er of Life   that   spark - les free,

Life . . . that flows for thee, . . Riv - er of Life . . . that all may
Riv - er of Life   that   flows for thee,   Riv - er of Life   that

see, . . . And dwell . . . on its banks for - ev - er.
all may see, And dwell on its banks for . . . ev - - er.

Copyright, 1889, by WM. J. KIRKPATRICK.

36

Keep in the Line.

Fanny J. Crosby.   Wm. J. Kirkpatrick.

1. Sol-diers for Je-sus, rise and a-way, Hark! 'tis the war-cry sound-ing to-day; Lo! our Command-er calls from the skies:
2. Sol-diers for Je-sus, hap-py are we; He our protect-or, near us will be, Trust in his mer-cy, change-less, di-vine;
3. Sol-diers for Je-sus, glad-ly we go, Smil-ing at dan-ger, brav-ing the foe, Bright are our landmarks, bright-ly they shine;
4. Sol-diers for Je-sus, vic-t'ry is nigh, Work till we gain it, rest by and by; Oh, let our cour-age nev-er de-cline;

CHORUS.

For-ward to conquest, lose not the prize! Now like an ar-my
March on with firmness, keep in the line.
March on re-joic-ing, keep in the line.
March on with boldness, keep in the line.

march-ing a-long, Fear-less and faith-ful, val-iant and strong,

Up with our banners, brightly they shine; March on together, keep in the line.

Copyright, 1886, by Wm. J. Kirkpatrick.

No Other Now.—CONCLUDED. 39

him I love to sing; No oth-er now but Je-sus, My Saviour and my King.

Hallelujah! Amen.

HENRIETTA E. BLAIR. Adapted and arr. by WM. J. KIRKPATRICK.

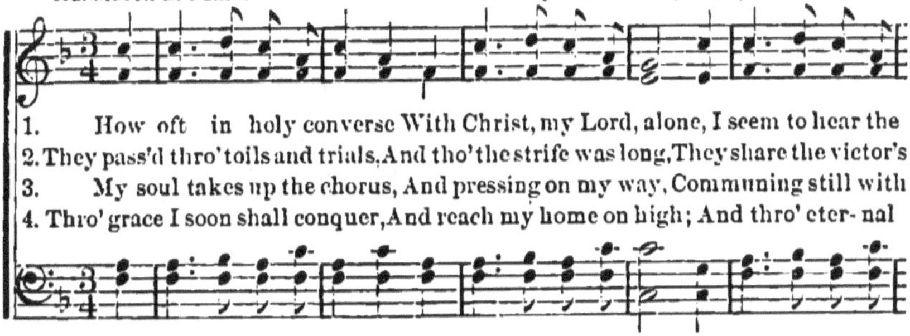

1. How oft in holy converse With Christ, my Lord, alone, I seem to hear the
2. They pass'd thro' toils and trials, And tho' the strife was long, They share the victor's
3. My soul takes up the chorus, And pressing on my way, Communing still with
4. Thro' grace I soon shall conquer, And reach my home on high; And thro' eter-nal

CHORUS.

millions That sing around his throne:— Hal-le-lu-jah, a-men. Halle-
conquest, And sing the victor's song.
Je-sus, I sing from day to day:
a-ges I'll shout beyond the sky:

poco rit.

lu-jah, A-men. Hal-le-lu-jah, A-men. A-men, A-men.

Copyright, 1885, by Wm. J. Kirkpatrick.

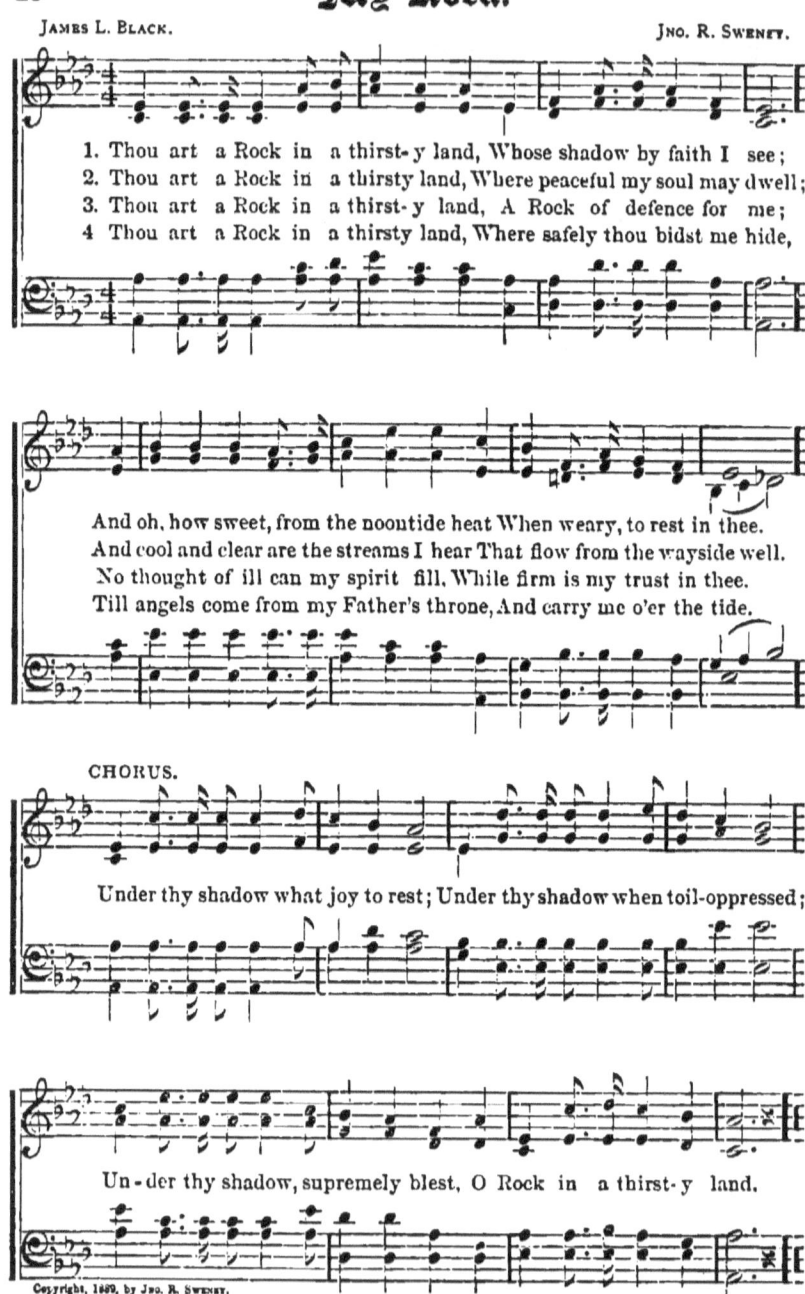

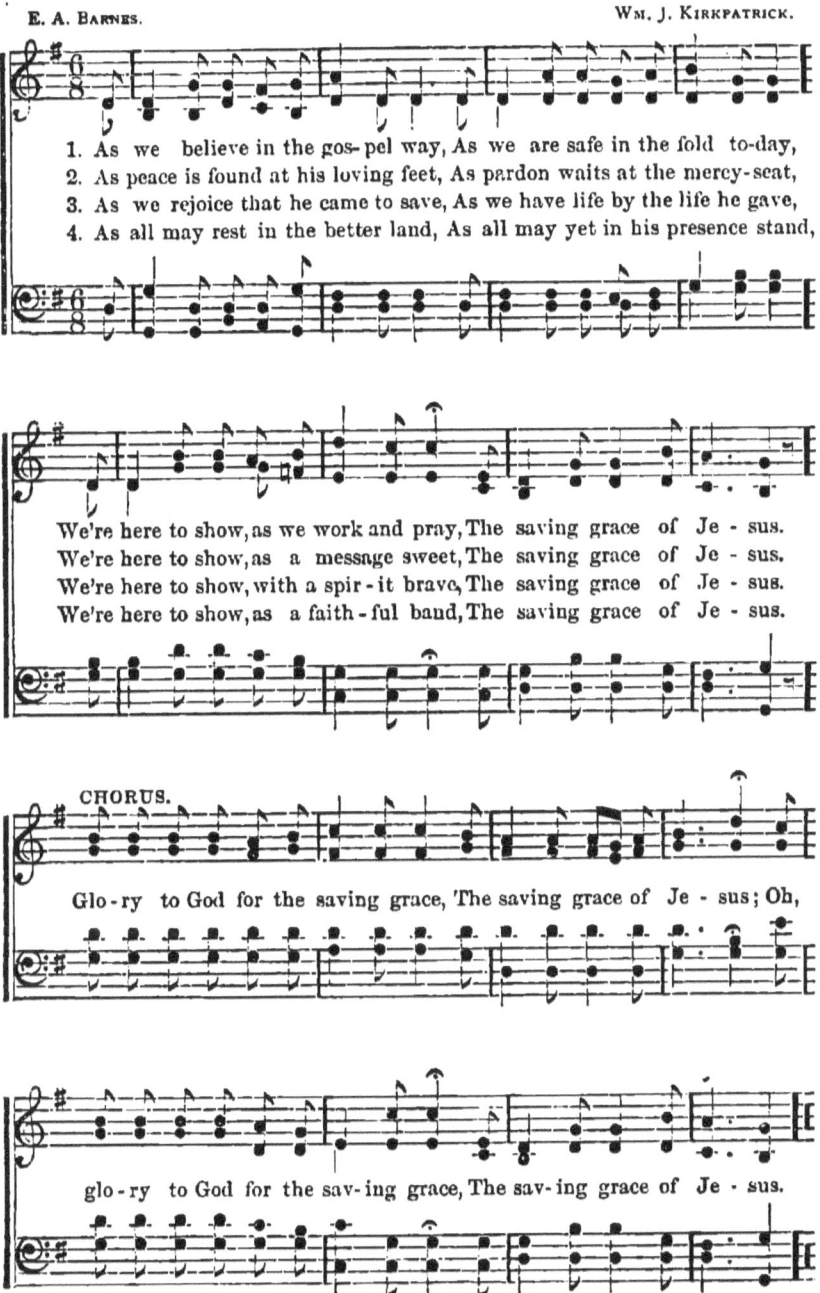

The Saving Grace of Jesus. 41

E. A. Barnes. Wm. J. Kirkpatrick.

1. As we believe in the gos-pel way, As we are safe in the fold to-day,
2. As peace is found at his loving feet, As pardon waits at the mercy-seat,
3. As we rejoice that he came to save, As we have life by the life he gave,
4. As all may rest in the better land, As all may yet in his presence stand,

We're here to show, as we work and pray, The saving grace of Je - sus.
We're here to show, as a message sweet, The saving grace of Je - sus.
We're here to show, with a spir - it brave, The saving grace of Je - sus.
We're here to show, as a faith - ful band, The saving grace of Je - sus.

CHORUS.

Glo - ry to God for the saving grace, The saving grace of Je - sus; Oh, glo - ry to God for the sav - ing grace, The sav - ing grace of Je - sus.

Copyright, 1890, by Wm. J. Kirkpatrick.

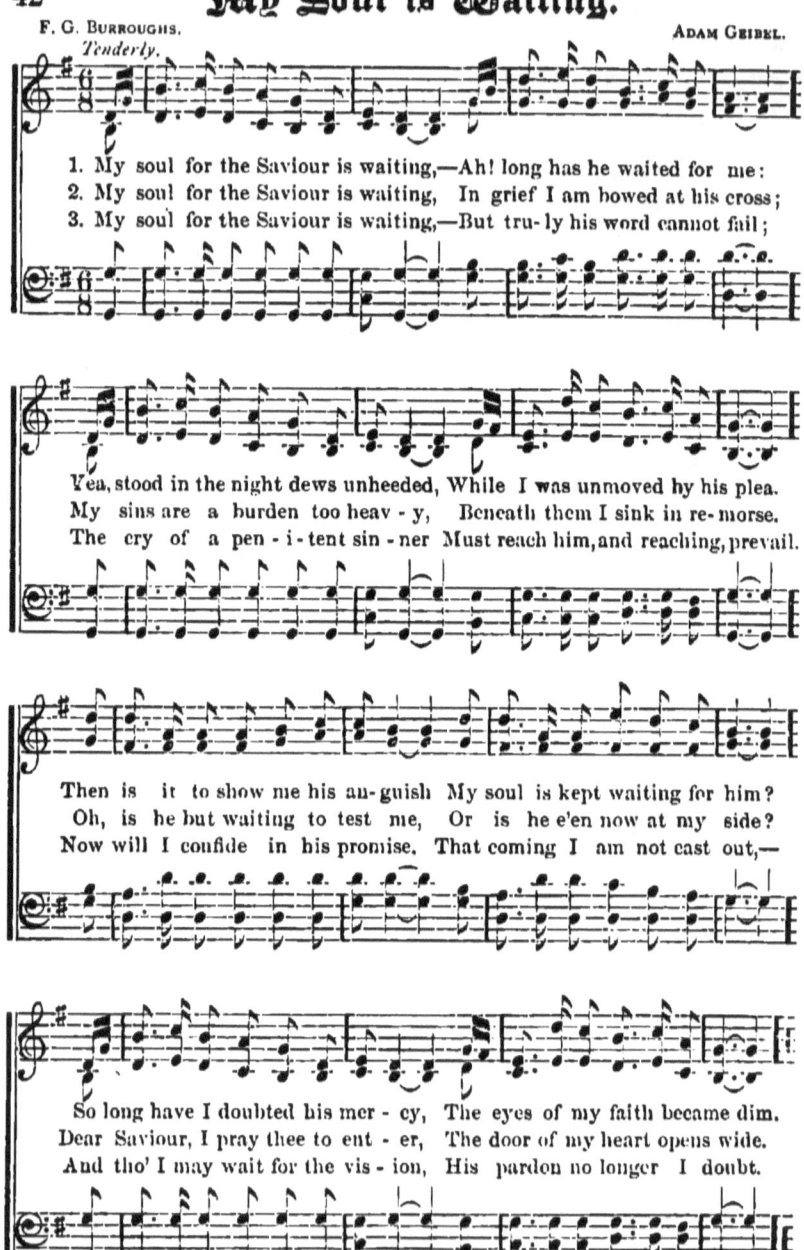

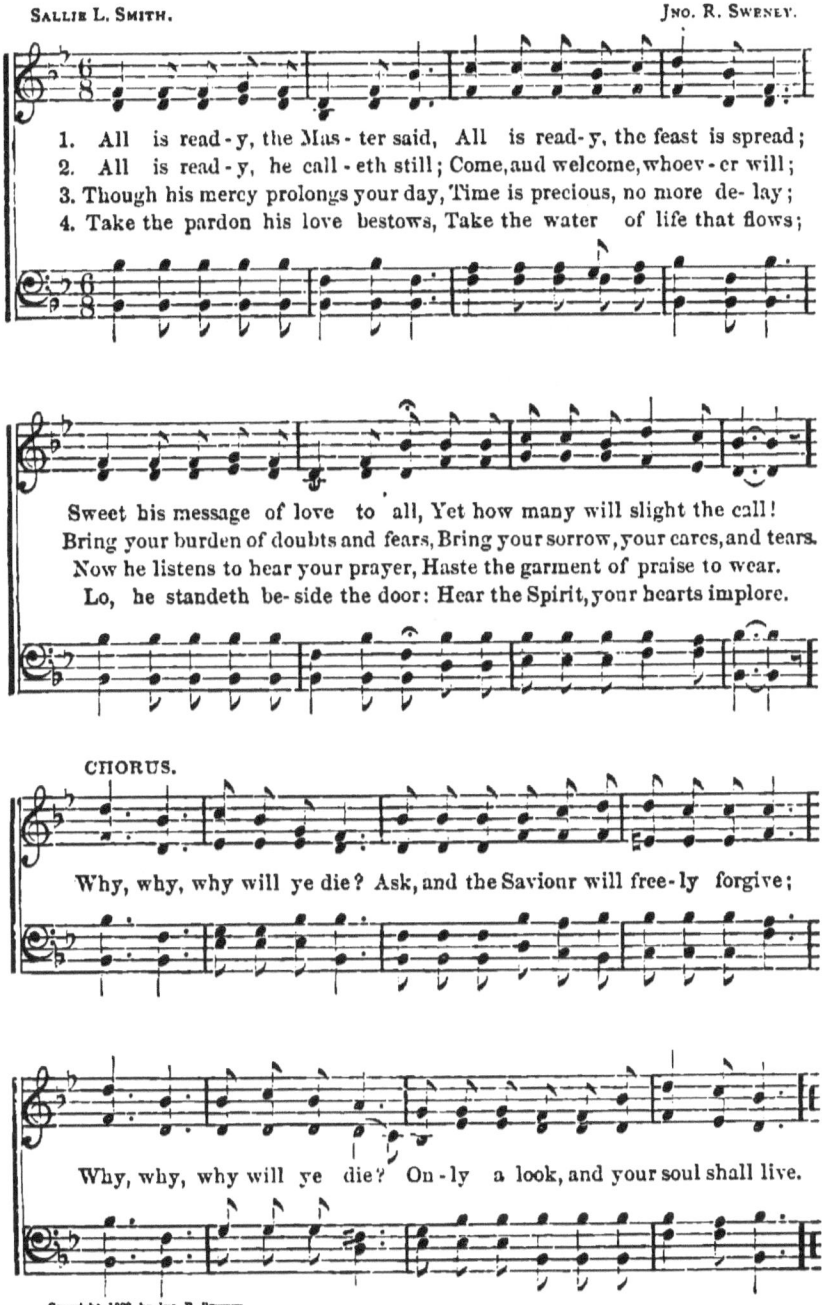

46. One in Thee.

LIZZIE EDWARDS. JNO R. SWENEY.

1. My faith, inspired with rapture, sings Thy grace, O Lord, to me;
2. The path of life and per-fect peace Thy grace unfolds to me;
3. I look be-yond the swelling tide, Where soon my rest will be;
4. And calm as now, with-out a storm, My clos-ing hour will be;

Thy grace, that saves from ev-'ry sin, And makes me one in thee.
No fear can harm, no care a-larm, For I am one in thee.
My hope is bright, my an-chor sure, For I am one in thee.
Thy grace will bring me safe-ly home, For I am one in thee.

CHORUS.

'Tis all of grace, thy gift so free,
'Tis all of grace, thy gift so free,

That I am one, O Lord, in thee.
That I am one, that I am one, O Lord, in thee.
That I am one, that I am one, O Lord, in thee.

Copyright, 1889, by Jno. R. Sweney.

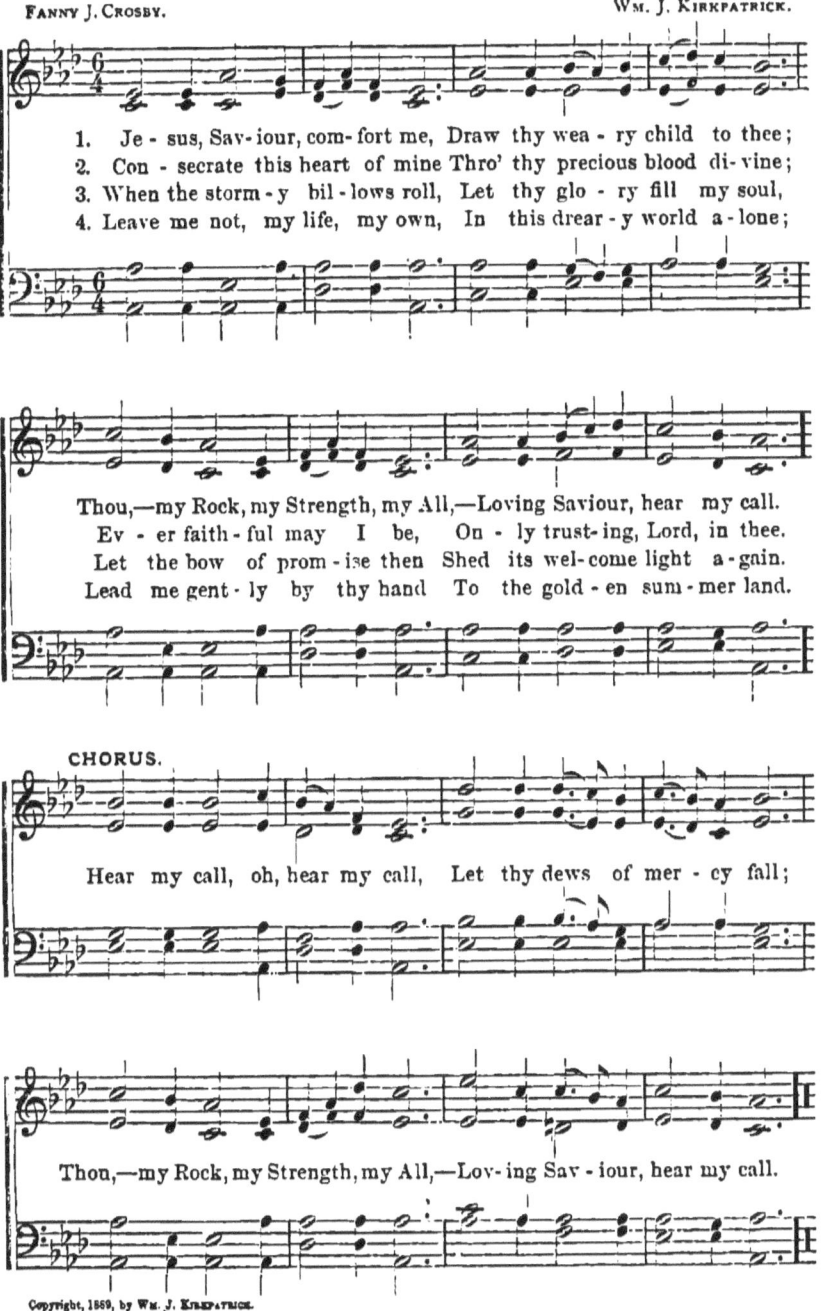

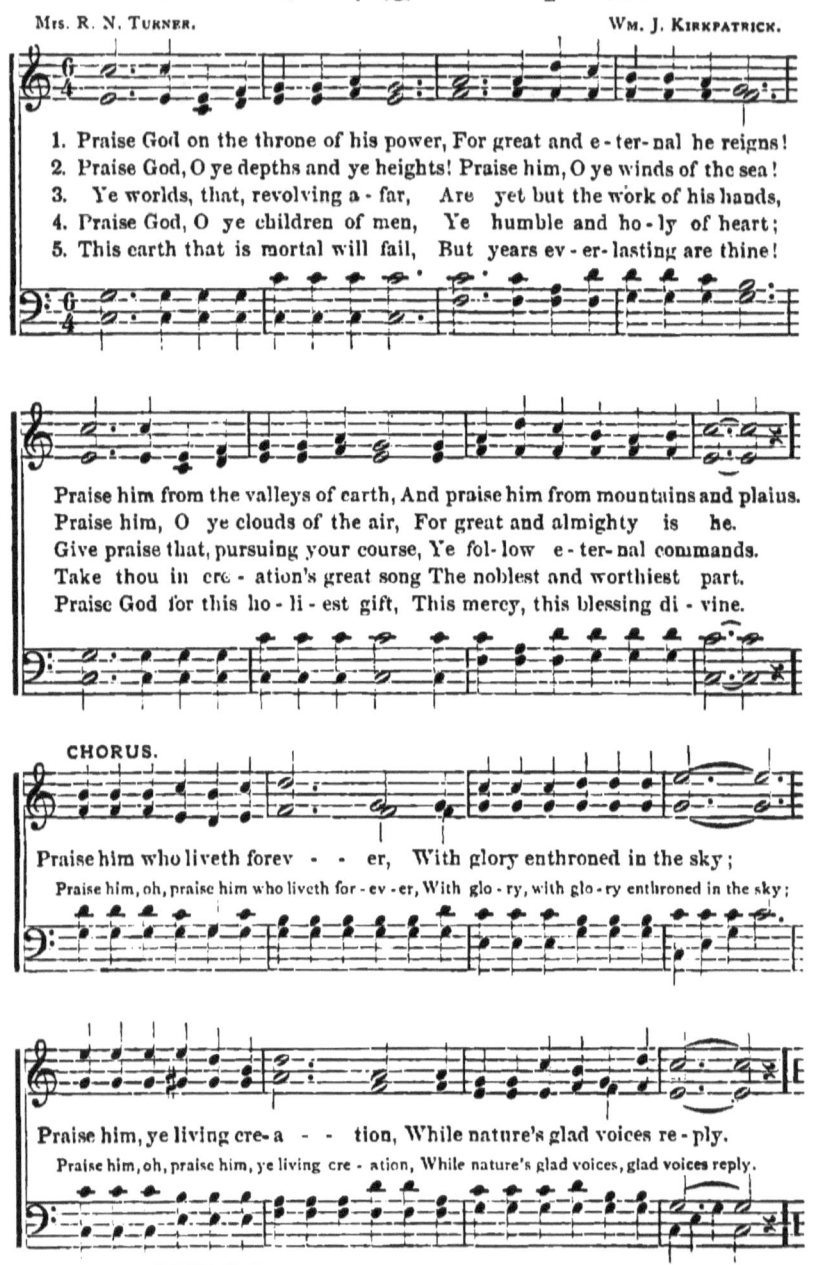

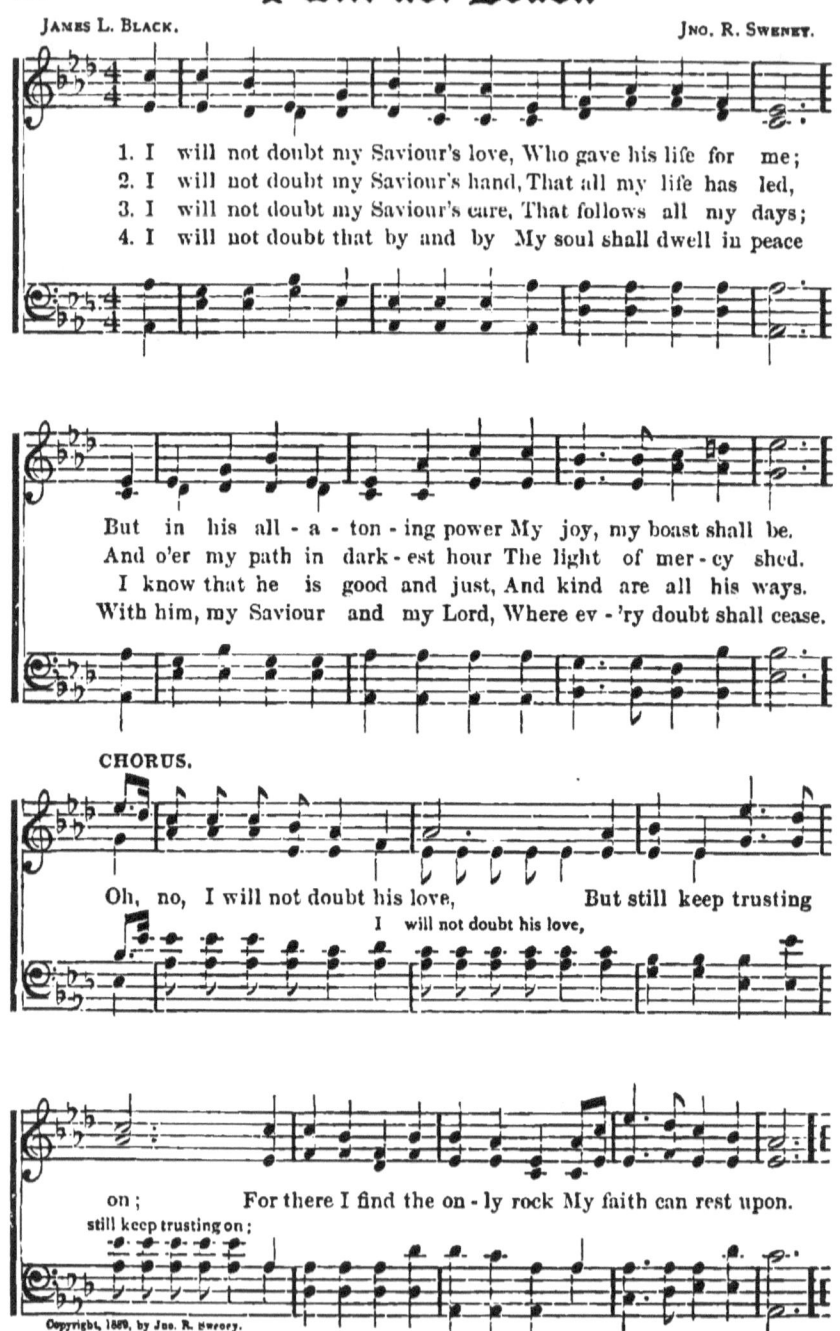

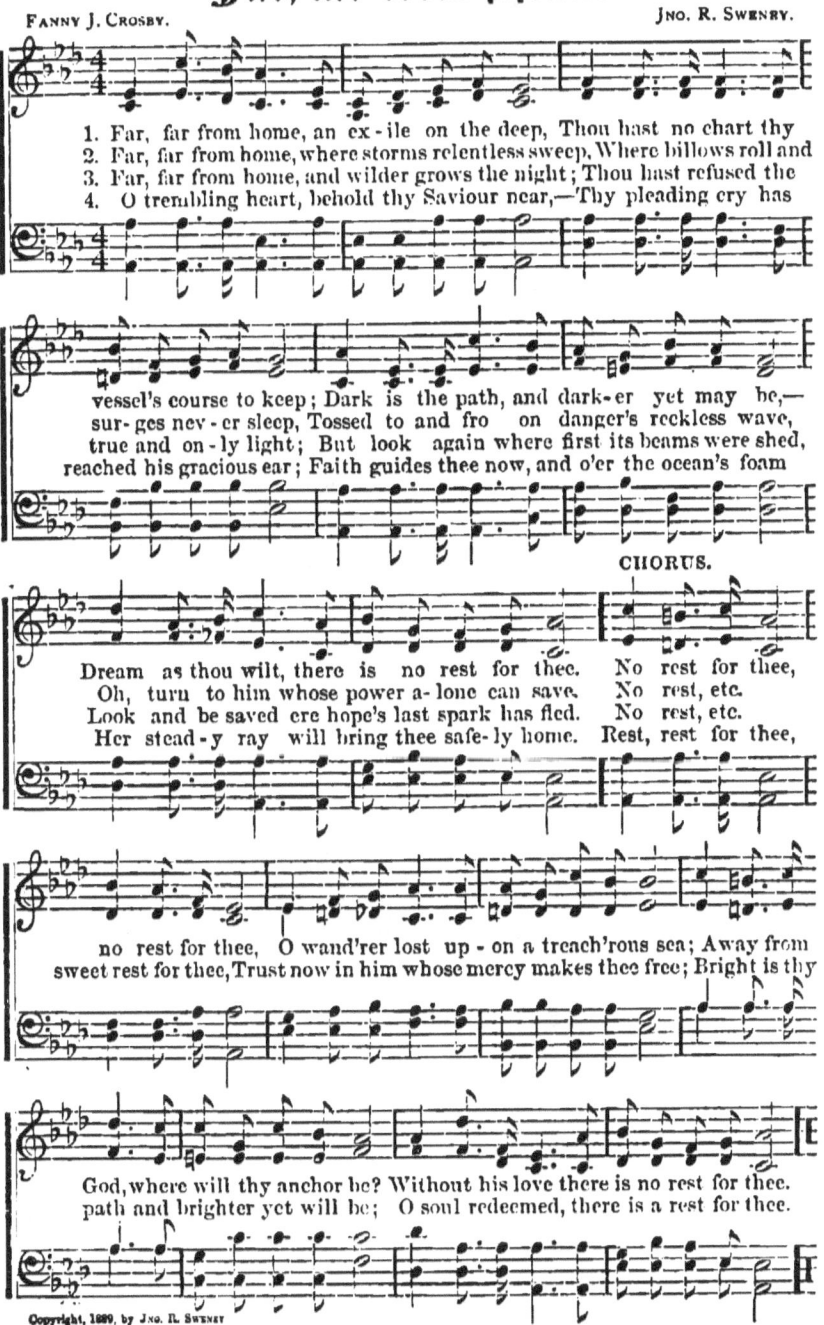

Our Fatherland.

FANNY J. CROSBY.   JNO. R. SWENEY.

1. Our Fatherland, thy name so dear Our souls repeat while strangers here;
2. Above the stars, above the skies, Thy tow'ring hills majestic rise;
3. There Jesus reigns, our Saviour-King, And one by one his own will bring,
4. No tears shall dim, no pain destroy The light of peace, the smile of joy;

And oh, how oft we sigh for thee, Our Father-land beyond the sea.
Thy sunny fields with verdure glow, And fadeless flowers in beauty grow.
Thy songs to join, thy bliss to share, O Father-land, our Zi-on fair.
No more we'll clasp the parting hand Within thy gates, our Father-land.

CHORUS.

Our Father-land, ... dear Father-land, ... We long to press . . . thy golden strand, . . . And hail the bright and shining

We long to press, we long to press thy golden strand.

Copyright, 1889, by JNO. R. SWENEY

Fresh Springs.

E. E. Hewitt. Wm. J. Kirkpatrick.

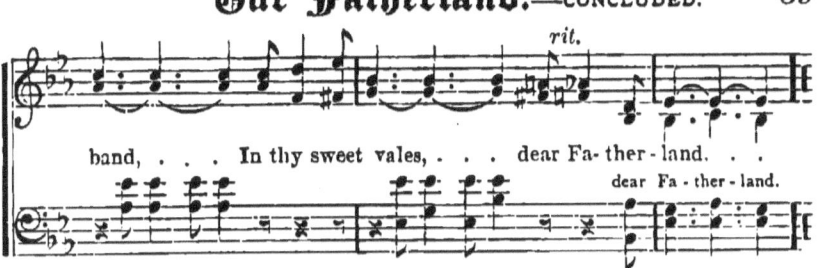

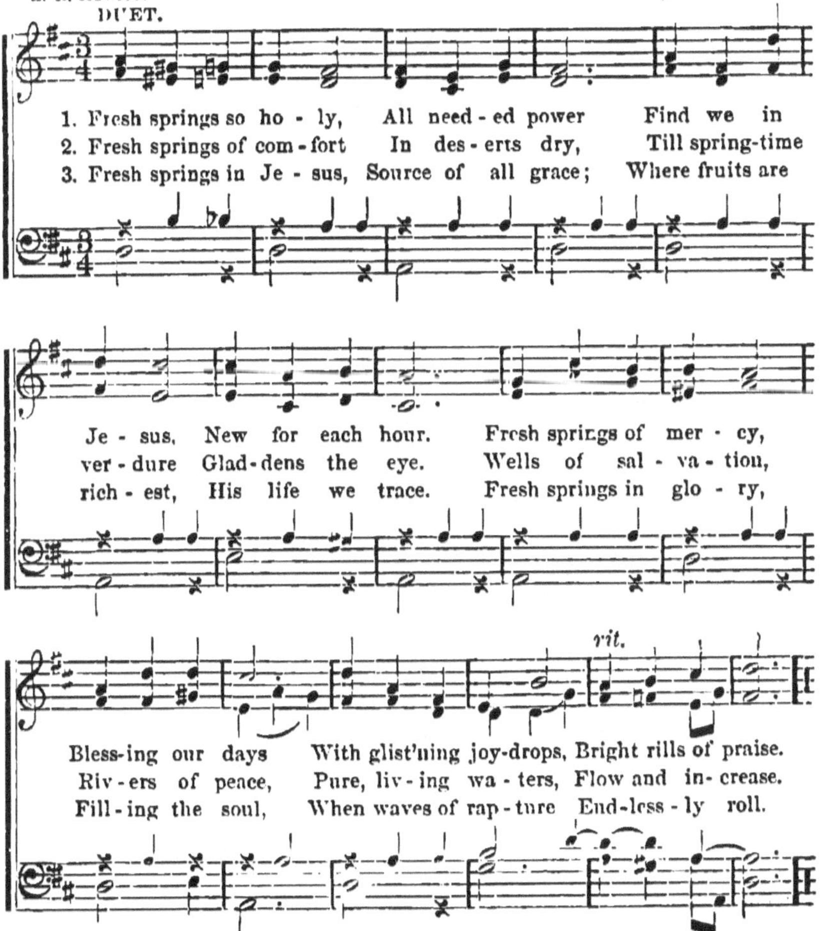

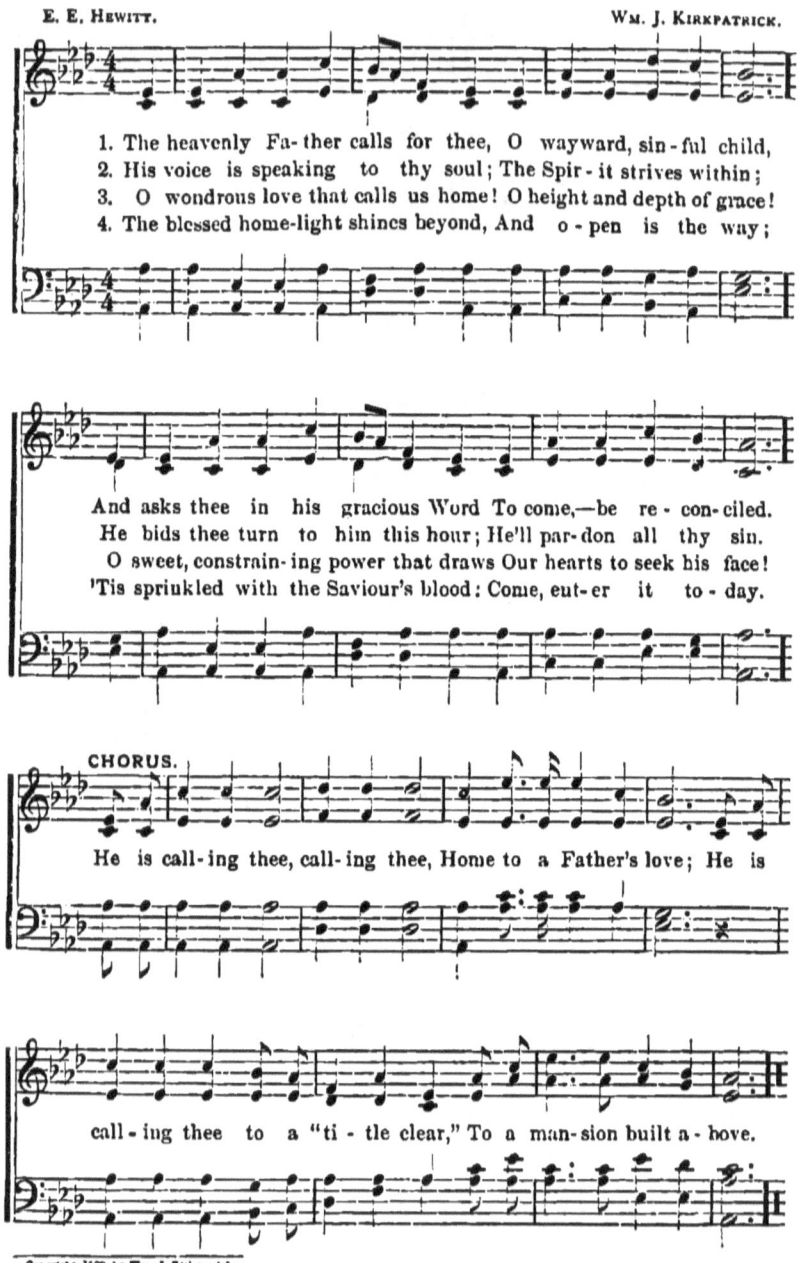

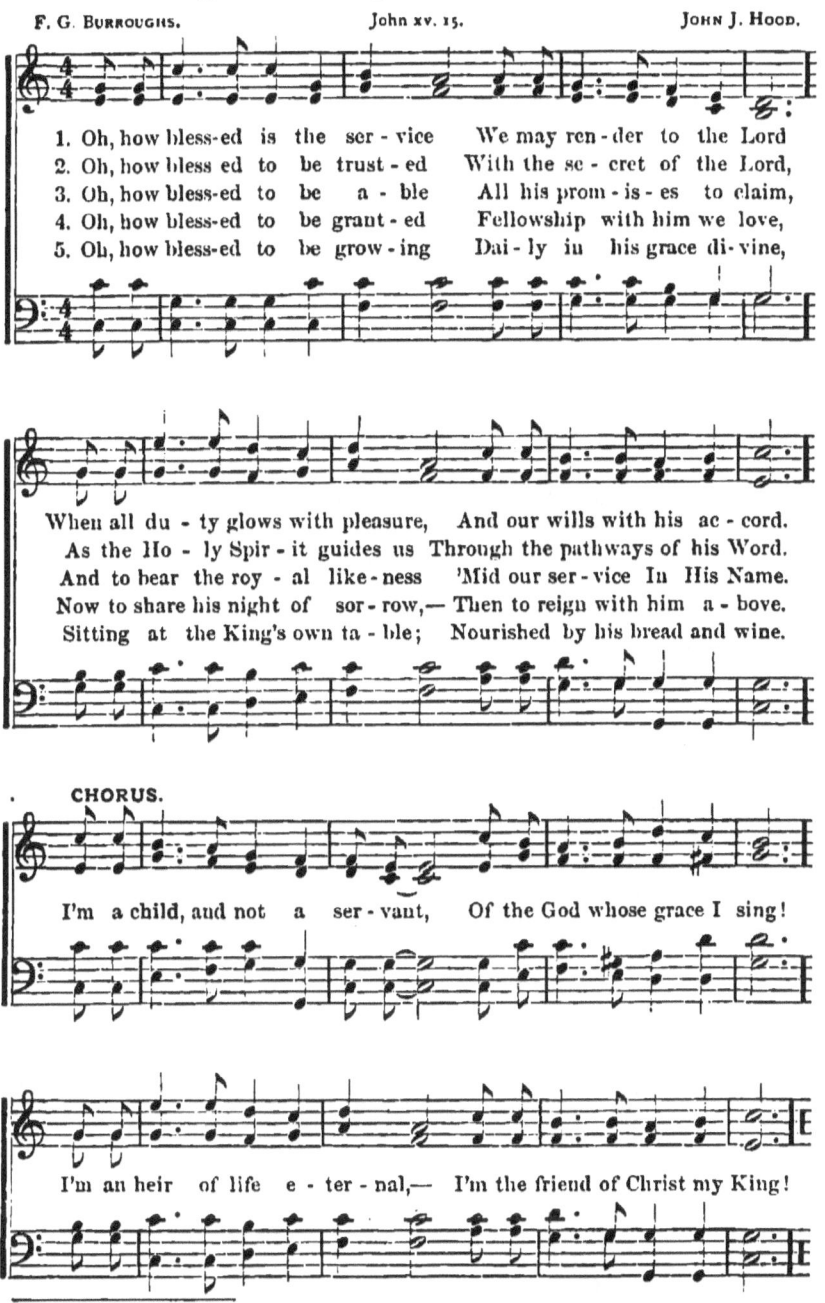

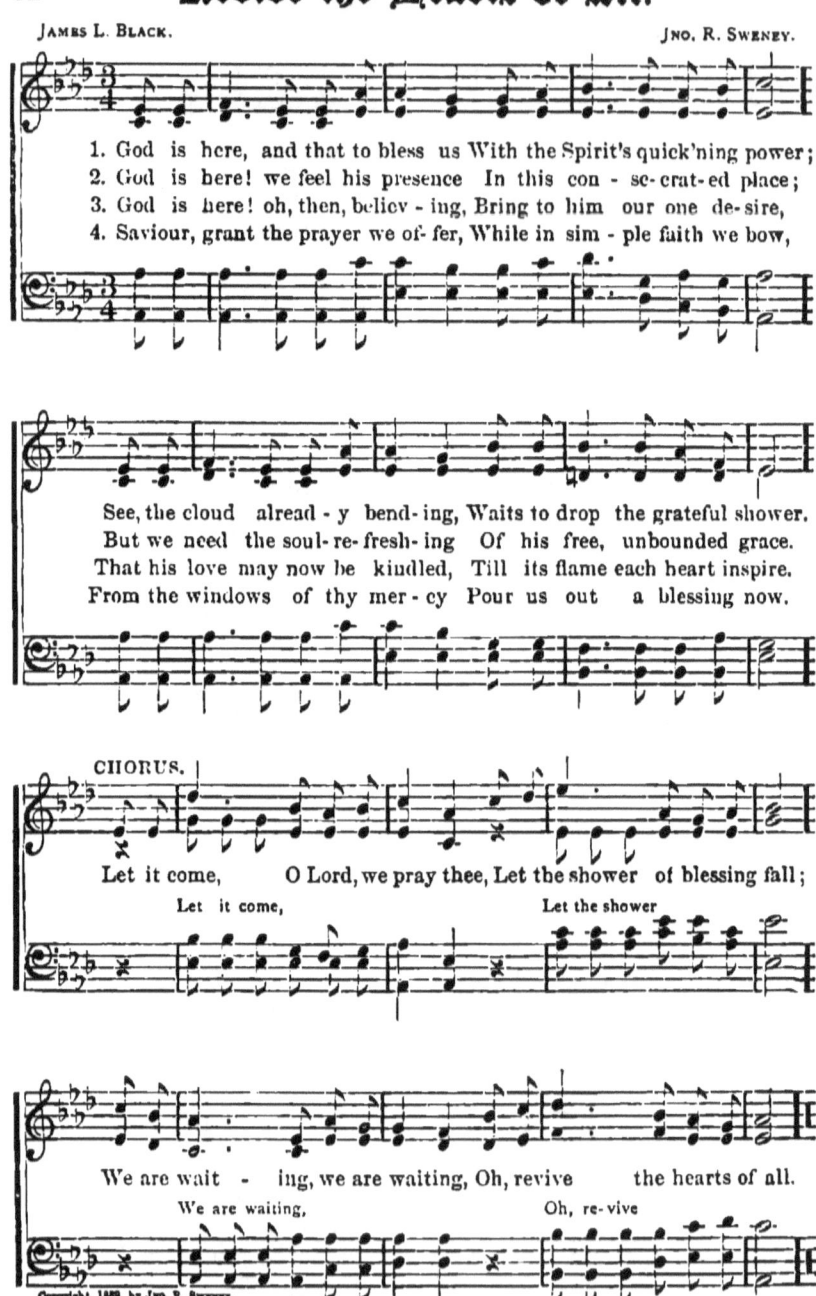

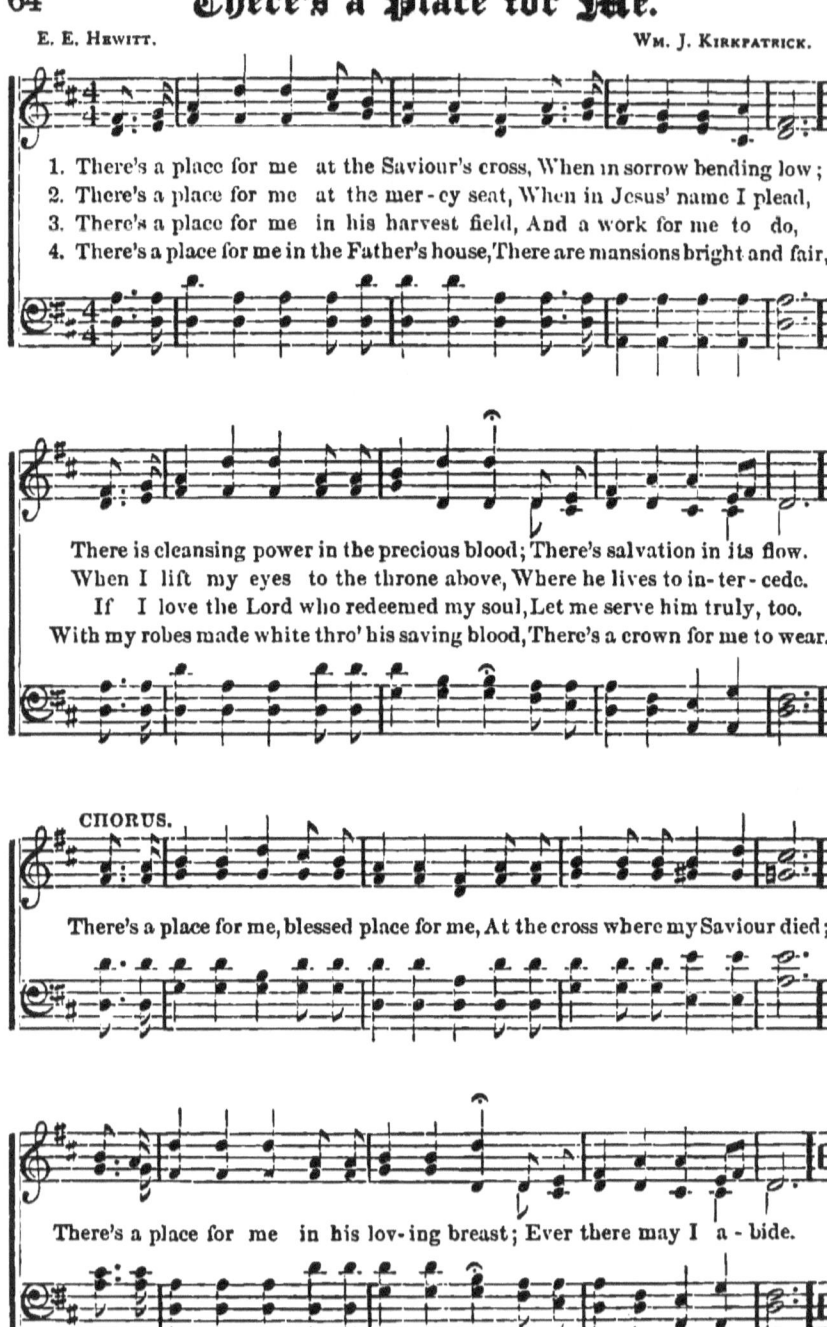

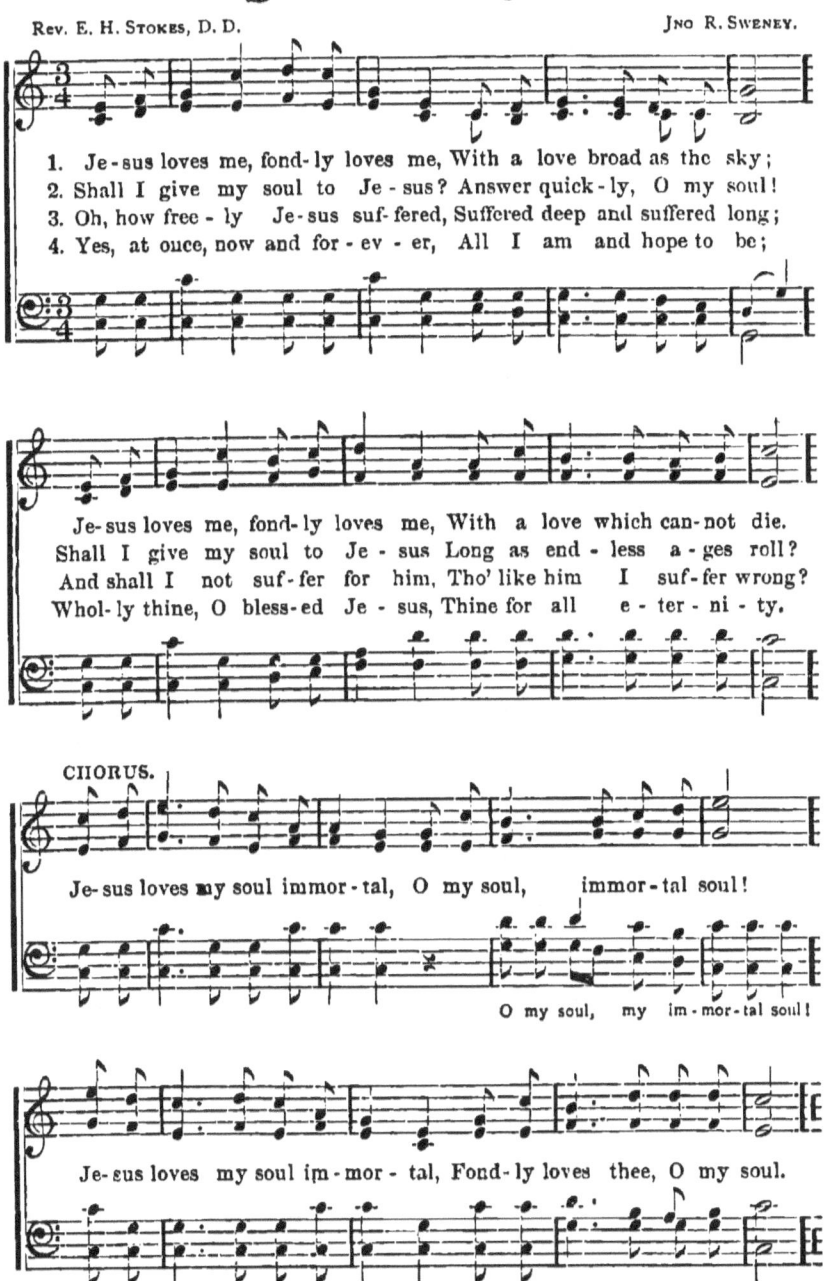

Tell it Out with Gladness.—CONCLUDED. 69

feel, Tell it out, tell it out with glad - ness.
world the joy you feel,

Holy Spirit.

L. W. MUNHALL. Jno. R. SWENEY.

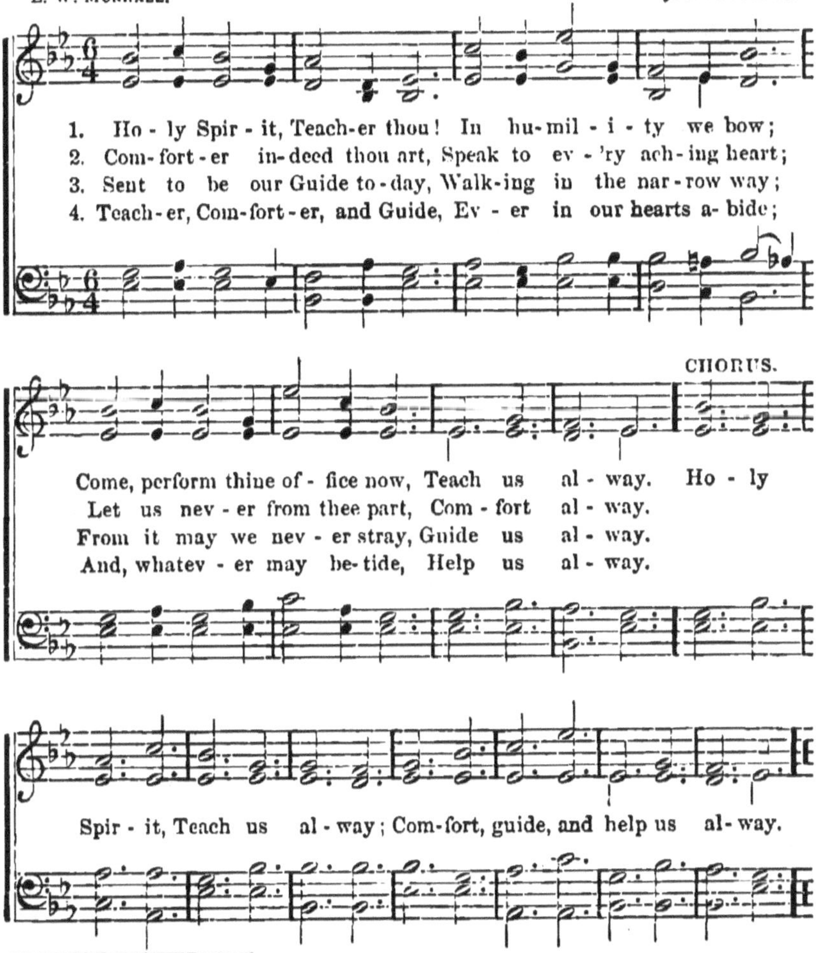

1. Ho - ly Spir - it, Teach-er thou! In hu-mil - i - ty we bow;
2. Com-fort-er in-deed thou art, Speak to ev - 'ry ach-ing heart;
3. Sent to be our Guide to-day, Walk-ing in the nar-row way;
4. Teach-er, Com-fort-er, and Guide, Ev - er in our hearts a-bide;

CHORUS.

Come, perform thine of - fice now, Teach us al - way. Ho - ly
Let us nev - er from thee part, Com - fort al - way.
From it may we nev - er stray, Guide us al - way.
And, whatev - er may be-tide, Help us al - way.

Spir - it, Teach us al - way; Com-fort, guide, and help us al - way.

Copyright, 1889, by Jno. R. Sweney.

72. There's a Hand Held Out.

M. W. Morse.
Jno. R. Sweney.

1. There's a hand held out in pi-ty, There's a hand held out in love; It will
2. Oh, how gently will it lead us! Oh, how tender is its touch! 'Tis the
3. Yes,'tis love to me, a sin-ner, Prompts this hand to reach so low, Striving
4. Shall I, to this hand extended, Pay no heed as it in-vites? Shall my

pi-lot to the ci-ty, Where our Father dwells a-bove.
bless-ed hand of Je-sus; We all need it, oh, so much!
thus to be the win-ner, Ere I reap what I shall sow.
Sav-iour be of-fend-ed, Give I not to him his rights?

CHORUS.

There's a hand held out to you, to you, There's a hand held out to me, to me,
There's a hand that will prove true, Whatev-er our lot shall be.

5 Nay, I would this proffered hand take,
    Knowing that it leads aright;
  Yes, I would this loving choice make;
    Trusting in his love and might.

6 Then, as hand in hand together
    With my Saviour, with my Friend,
  With my Christ, my Elder Brother,
    Let him lead till life shall end.

Copyright, 1890, by Jno. R. Sweney.

Stepping-stones to Jesus. 73

E. E. Hewitt.
Wm. J. Kirkpatrick.

Moderato.

1. Stepping-stones to Je-sus All our joys may be, Used with glad thanksgiving
2. Stepping-stones to Je-sus, Leading to his feet, Are the lit-tle tri-als,
3. Stepping-stones to Je-sus, All the pure delight In his works of beauty,
4. Stepping-stones to Jesus, Blessed means of grace; Prayer and sweet communion

For his love so free. Many, many blessings In our pathway fall, Stepping-stones to
Which we daily meet; Ev'ry need that presses, Ev'ry vexing care, Ev'ry dis-ap-
All things fair and bright. Ev'ry sweet affection, Tender human love, Brought in conse-
In the sacred place; Ev'ry self-denial For the Master's cause, Each renewed o-

CHORUS.

Jesus We may find them all. Looking for the stepping-stones
pointment, Ev'ry cross we bear. Placed along life's way;
cration To the Friend above.
beying Of his ho-ly laws.

Looking for the stepping-stones, We find them ev'ry day; Stepping-stones to Jesus,

p   *poco rit.*   *ad lib.*

Stepping-stones to Jesus, Looking for the stepping-stones, We find them ev'ry day.

Copyright, 1889, by Wm J. Kirkpatrick

5 I dreamed that hoary time had fled,
　And earth and sea gave up their dead,
　A fire dissolved this ball,
I saw the church's ransomed throng,
I heard the burden of their song,
　'Twas "Christ is all in all."

6 Then come to Christ, oh, come to-day,
　The Father, Son, and Spirit say;
　The Bride repeats the call,
For he will cleanse your guilty stains,
His love will soothe your weary pains,
　For "Christ is all in all."

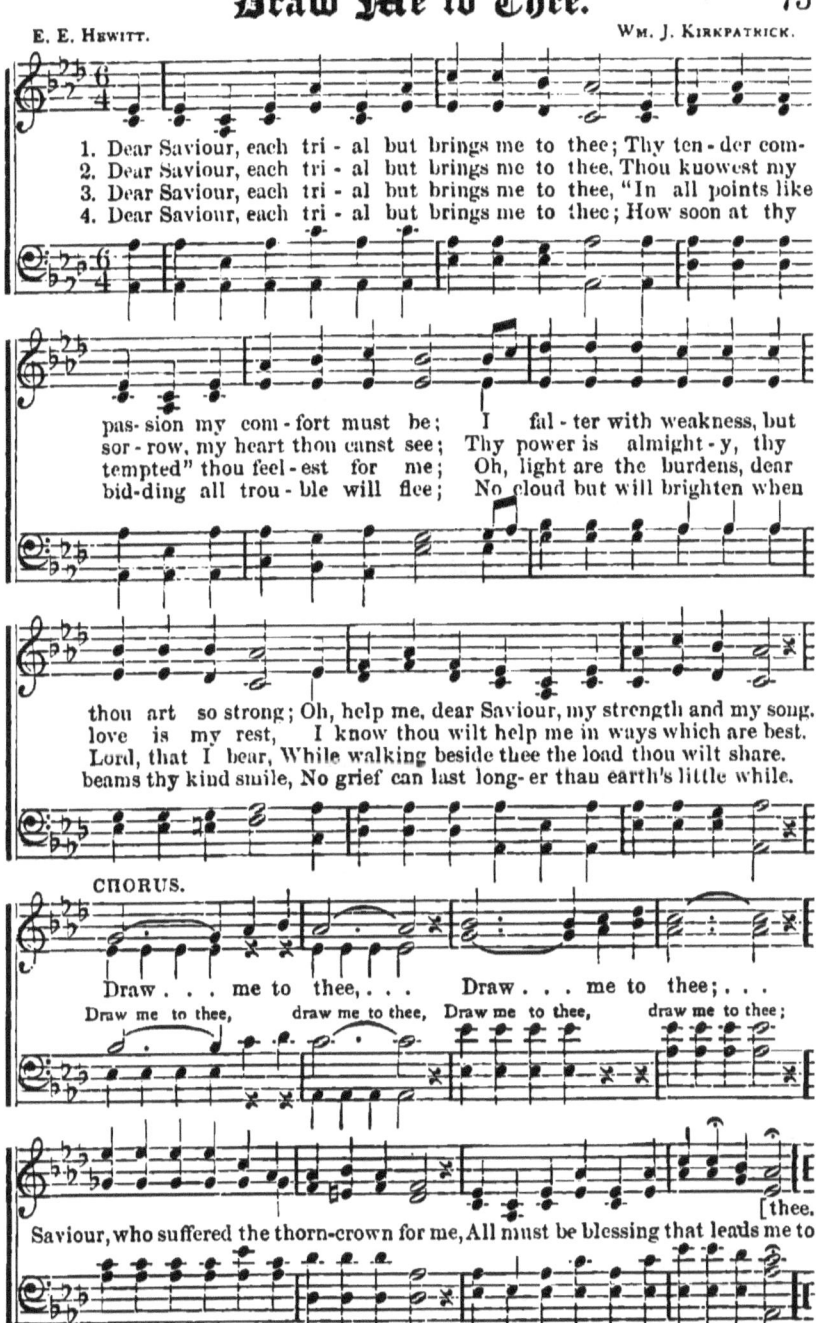

What will the First Greeting be?

P. H. DINGMAN. JNO. R. SWENEY.

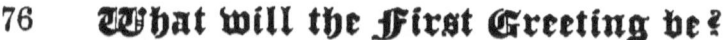

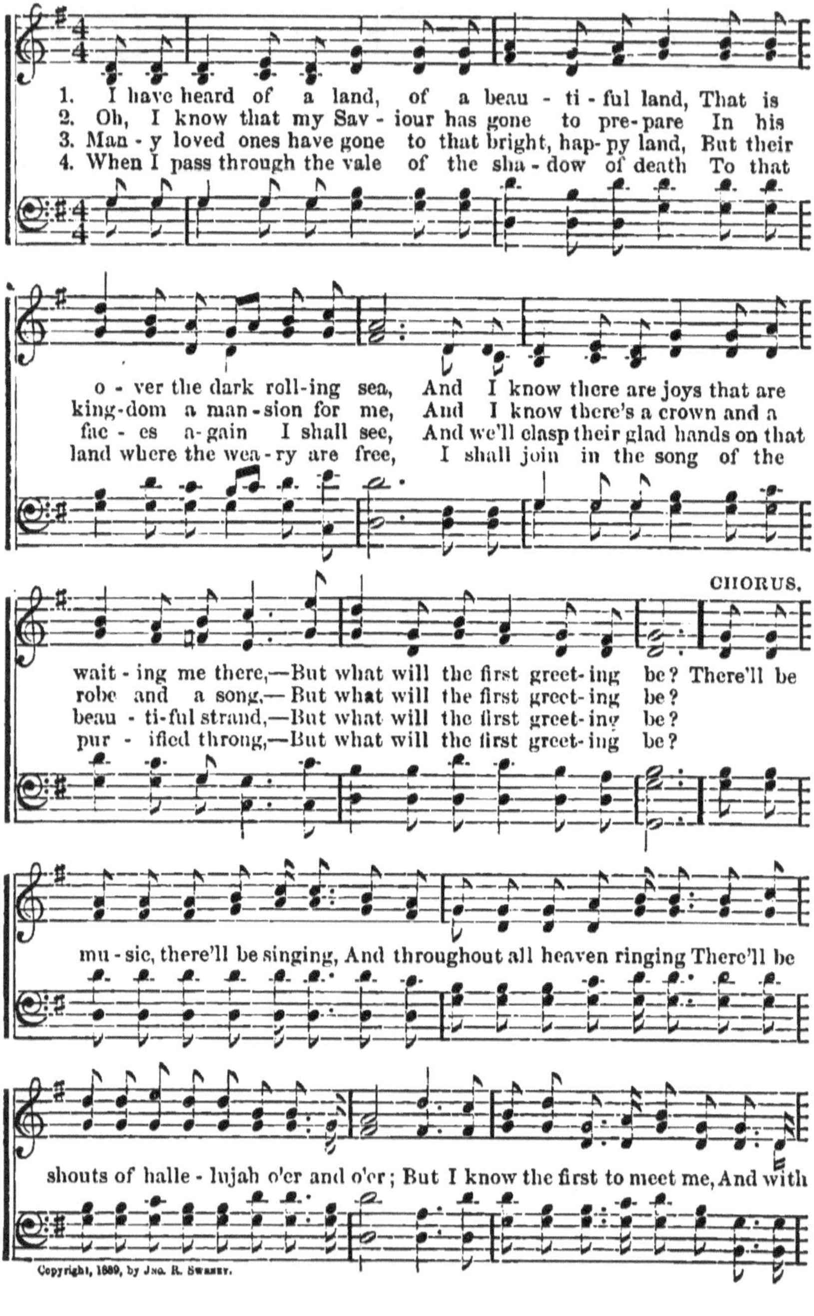

Since I Have Been Redeemed. 79

E. O. E.   F. O. EXCELL. By per.

1. I have a song I love to sing, Since I have been redeemed, Of my Re-
2. I have a Christ that satis-fies, Since I have been redeemed, To do his
3. I have a Witness bright and clear, Since I have been redeemed, Dispelling
4. I have a joy I can't express, Since I have been redeemed, All thro' his
5. I have a home prepared for me, Since I have been redeemed, Where I shall

CHORUS.

deemer, Saviour King, Since I have been redeemed. Since I . . . have been re-
will my highest prize, Since I have been redeemed.
every doubt and fear, Since I have been redeemed.
blood and righteousness, Since I have been redeemed.
dwell e-ter-nal-ly, Since I have been redeemed. Since I have been redeemed, since

deemed,   Since I have been redeemed, I will glory in his name, Since
I have been redeemed,

I . . . . have been redeemed,   I will glory in the Saviour's name.
I have been redeemed, since I have been redeemed,

Copyright, 1884, by E. O. Excell.

4 But God has given us the now,—
 The past himself will take;
And if to him in faith we go
 He'll save, for Jesus' sake.

5 No matter what thy past may be,
 Just leave that all with Christ;
He knows it all, yet calleth thee,
 And bids thee dare to trust.

Give Thanks.—CONCLUDED. 83

For his mercy en-dur-eth for-ev - er, O give thanks, O give thanks.

Work, oh, Work for Jesus.

E. E. HEWITT.   JNO. R. SWENEY.

1. Work, oh, work for Jesus; in his blessed ser-vice There is room for all;
2. Work, oh, work for Jesus; tho' it be in weakness, Claim his mighty power;
3. Work, oh, work for Jesus, tho' thy field of labor Small and humble be;
4. Work, oh, work for Jesus, for each faithful servant His reward shall share;

Something for the youngest, something for the oldest; Who will heed his call?
He can give us counsel, give us faith and courage, For each try-ing hour.
There, until the Master bids thee "come up higher," Serve him patiently.
Happy, happy entrance to the Royal Pal-ace, Crowns of glo-ry there!

CHORUS.

Work, work for Jesus, heed the Master's cry;
Work, work for Jesus, the hours are flitting by;

Broad the fields of harvest, see how white they lie: Work, go work to-day.

Copyright, 1889, by Jno. R. Sweney.

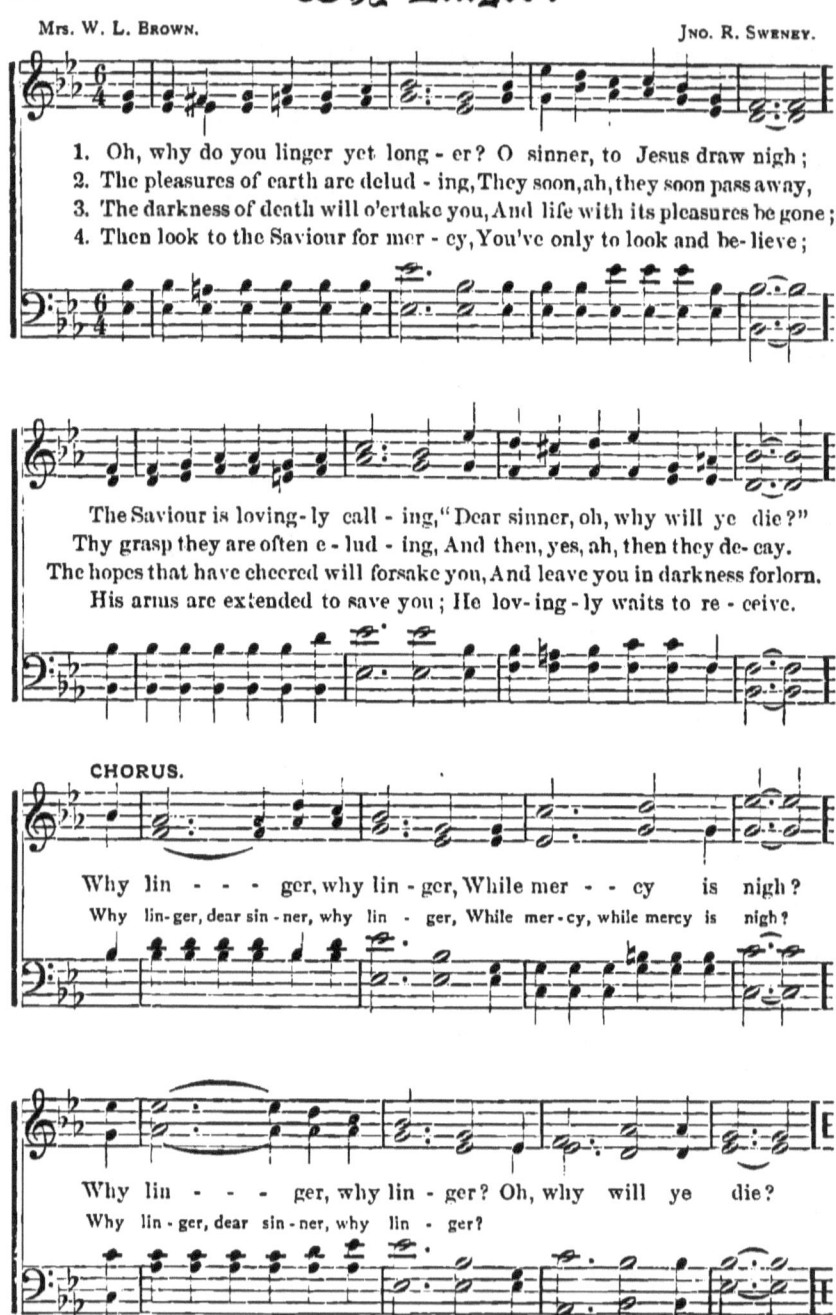

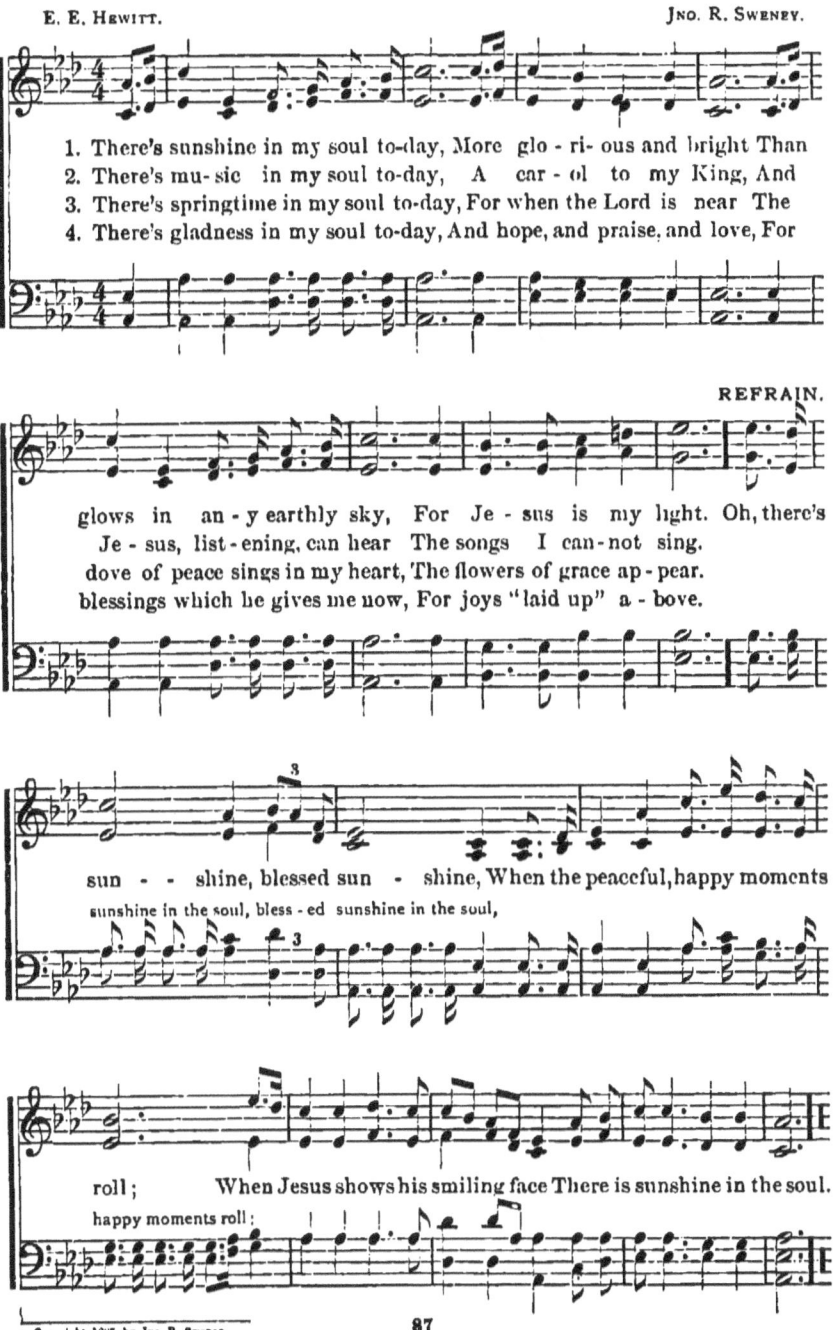

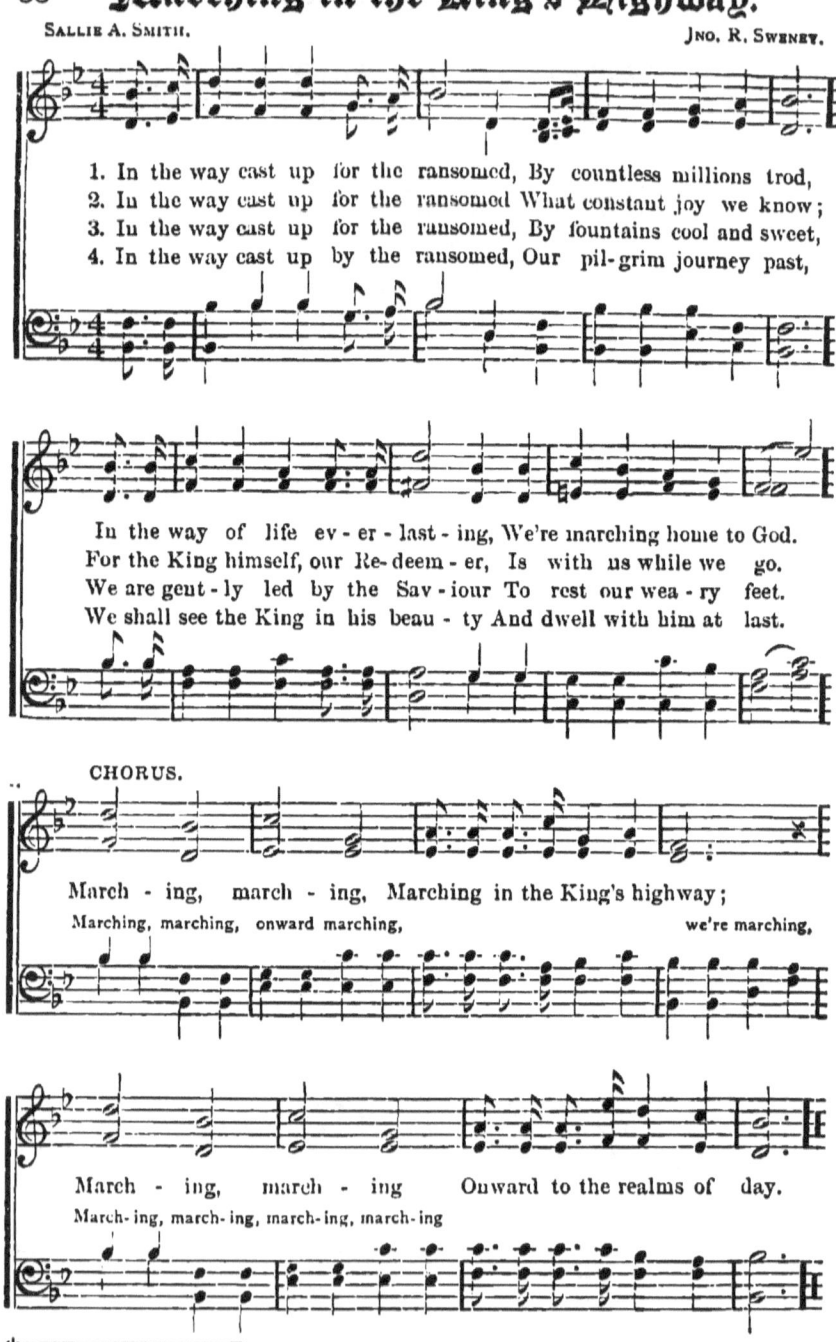

God's Word. 89

M. L. Munhall.
Wm. J. Kirkpatrick.

1. The Bi-ble was giv-en That lost men may know The way in-to heav-en, And shun hell be-low. It does not de-ceive us; Is faith-ful to tell Of sin, death, and judgment, And torments of hell.
2. It then points to Je-sus, Redeem-er of all, The mighty who frees us From curse of the fall. It shows us our du-ty To God and to man In words of great beauty, And know them all can.
3. It tells us of heav-en, The home of the soul, And crowns to be giv-en, While ag-es shall roll. Oh, heav-en-born trea-sure! We would have the more, In ful-ness of measure And richness of store.

CHORUS.

No word ev-er spo-ken By God to his own
No word ev-er spoken By God to his own, No word ev-er spoken By God to his own

Was ev - - er yet bro - ken; 'Tis firm as his throne.
Was ev-er yet broken, Was ev-er yet broken; 'Tis firm, 'tis firm as his throne.

Copyright, 1889, by Wm J. Kirkpatrick

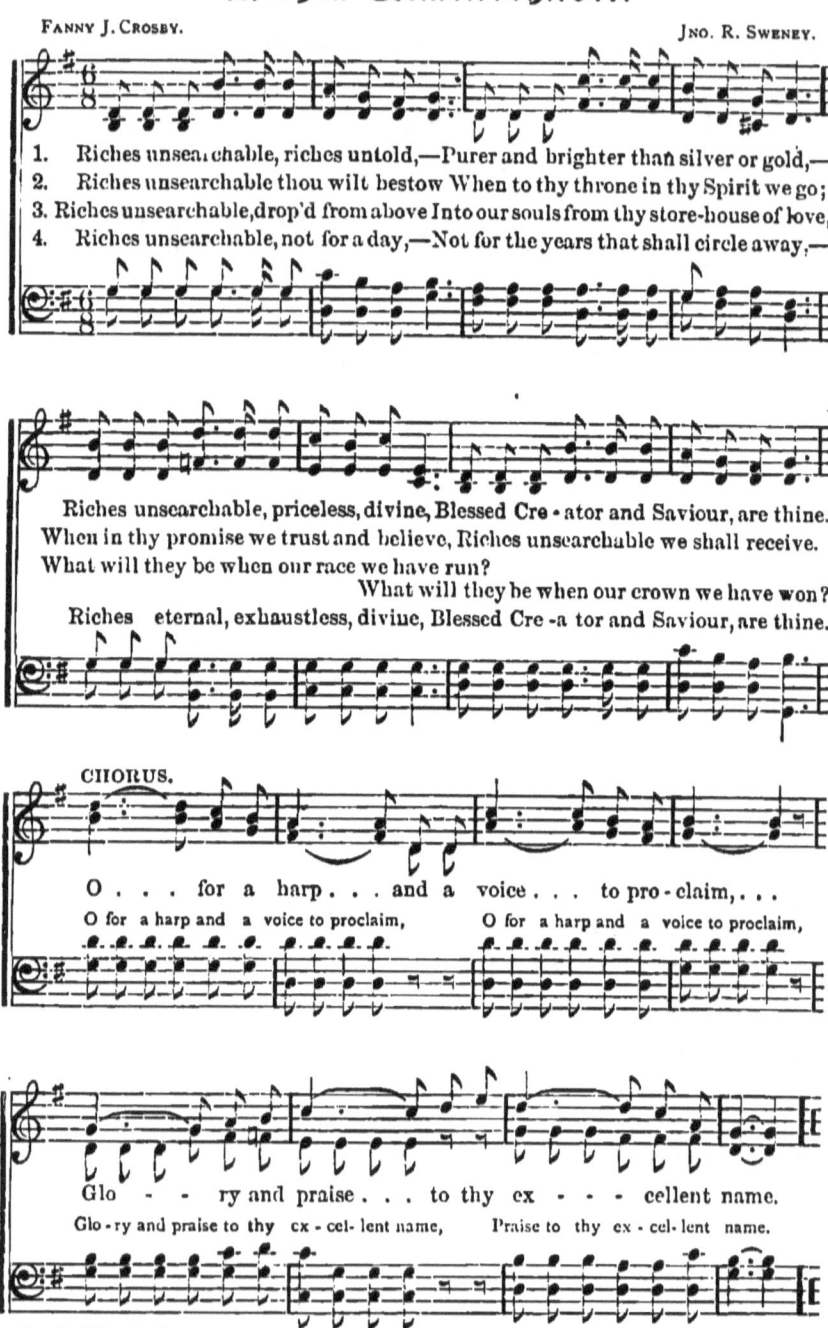

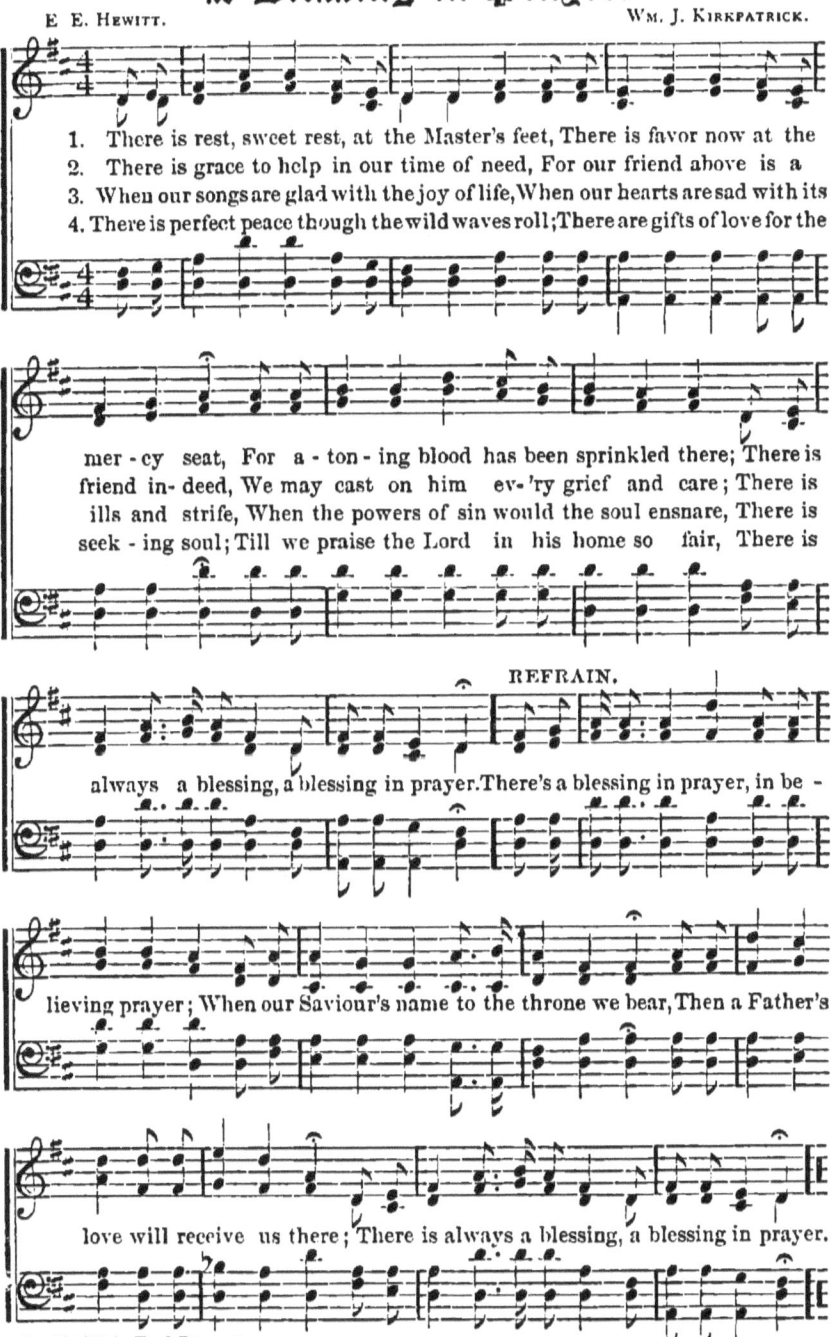

94. All Things are Mine.

E. A. Barnes.   Jno. R. Sweney.

1. 'Tis mine to walk in the nar-row way, With Je-sus for a guide;
2. 'Tis mine to know, in its rich sup-ply, The fullness of his love;
3. 'Tis mine to watch for the coming Lord, While waiting in this vale;

'Tis mine to stand in his strength to-day, Whatev-er may be-tide;
'Tis mine to hold as the days pass by The faith that looks a-bove;
'Tis mine to rest in the promised word, And know it will not fail;

'Tis mine to have in my dai-ly life, His Spir-it sweet and free:
'Tis mine to have, 'mid the storms of life, A Ref-uge near and strong:
'Tis mine to rise at the fin-al day, E-ter-nal things to see:

Yes, free-ly mine are these gifts divine, Thro' Christ who died for me.
Yes, free-ly mine are these gifts divine, Thro' Christ my shield and song.
Yes, free-ly mine are these gifts divine, Thro' Christ who died for me.

CHORUS.

All things are mine, halle-lu-jah! Free-ly mine, free-ly mine;

Copyright, 1880, by Jno. R. Sweney.

All Things are Mine.—CONCLUDED. 95

All things are mine! oh, rejoice and sing! Now and forever all are mine.

Lead Me, Precious Saviour.

Mrs. J. F. K.   Mrs. Jos. F. Knapp. By per.

1. Lead me, lead me, Lead me, precious Saviour, In- to the narrow way, In-
2. I will love thee, Ev- er, ev- er love thee; May sinful thoughts depart, Oh,
3. Lead me, fold me, Guide, and ever keep me, And thanks my heart will give, Dear

CHORUS.

to the narrow way, Fold me, fold me, Fold me to thy bo-som, And
take them from my heart.
Saviour, while I live.

may I never stray, oh, nev - er stray, And I will praise thee ev - ermore, yes,

ev - er - more, And I will praise thee ev - ermore, yes, ev - er - more.

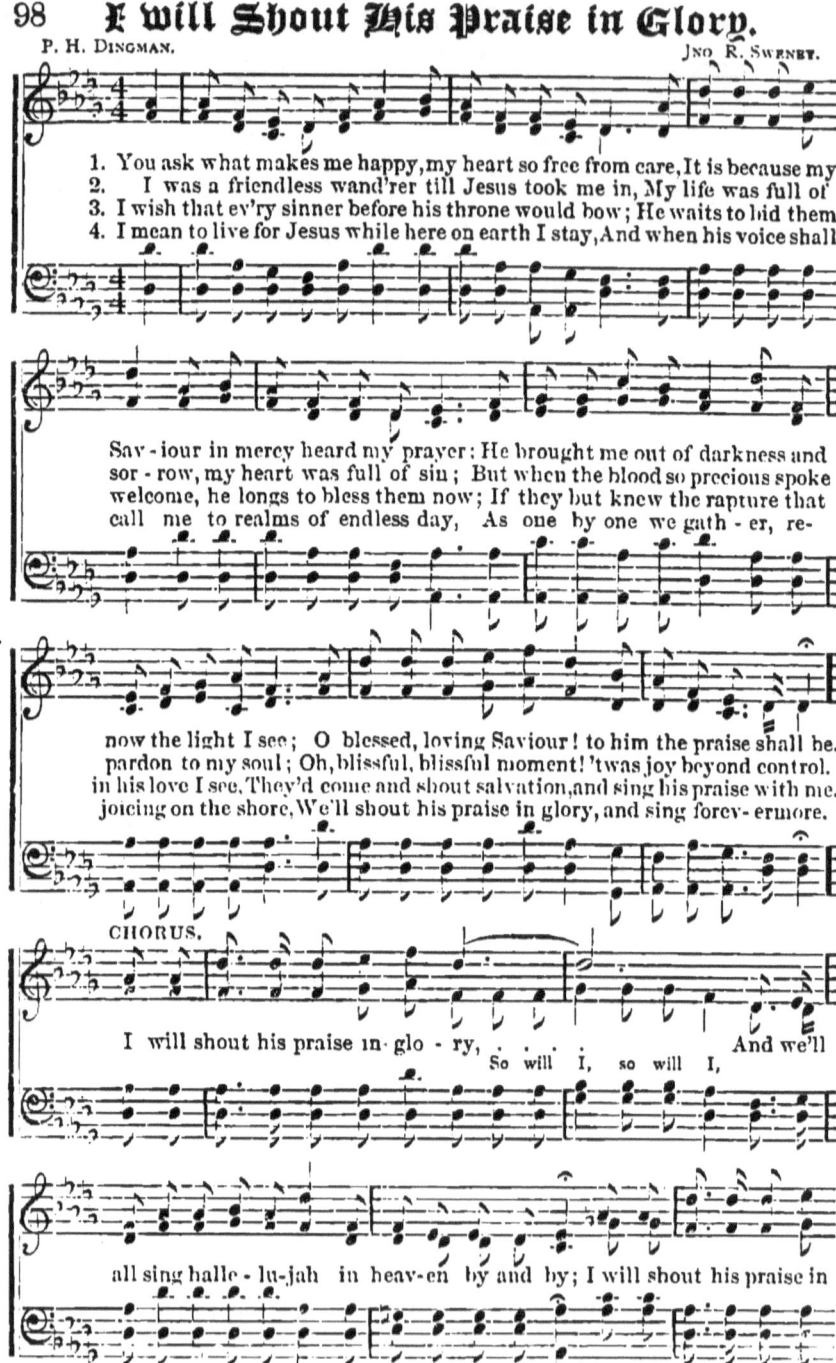

102. Oh, Praise His Name Forever.

E. R. Latta.   Wm. J. Kirkpatrick.

1. Oh, praise his name for-ev-er! The wondrous sto-ry tell, He laid a-side his glo-ry In human form to dwell; Up-on the world's re-demp-tion The an-gels gaze in vain, But to repentant sin-ners The Spir-it makes it plain.

2. Oh, praise his name for-ev-er! His life and death be-hold! Of all his love and pi-ty How lit-tle can be told! Oh, sin-ner, will you own him, That he may ransom thee? Or will you still de-ny him, And lost for-ev-er be?

3. Oh, praise his name for-ev-er! My glad, triumphant soul, By him set free from bondage, By him from sin made whole; When I have earth for-sak-en, And gained the further shore, I'll tell the sto-ry bet-ter, I'll praise him ev-er-more.

CHORUS.

Oh, praise his name for-ev-er, Praise his ho-ly name; His goodness fail-eth nev-er, Praise his ho-ly name.

Copyright, 1881, by John J. Hood.

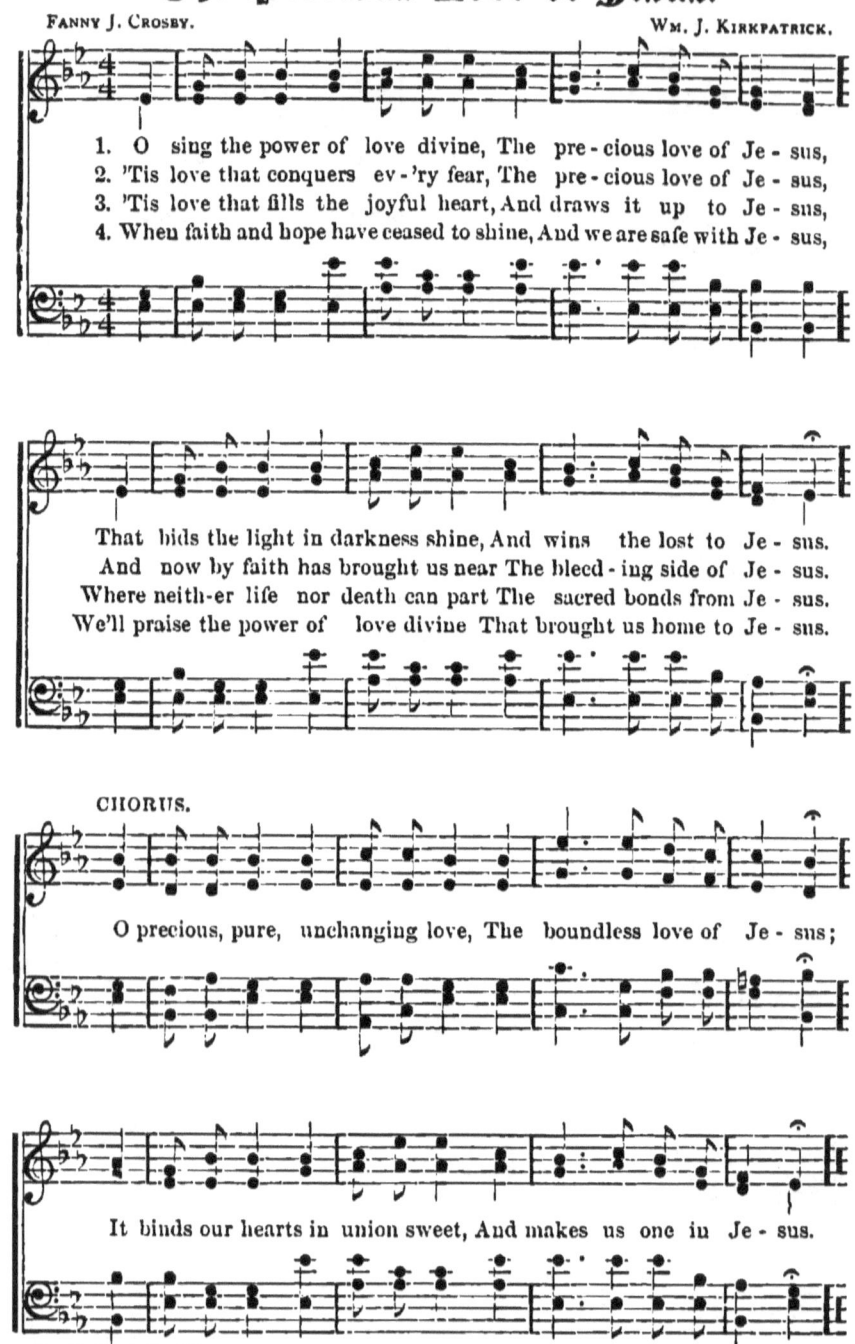

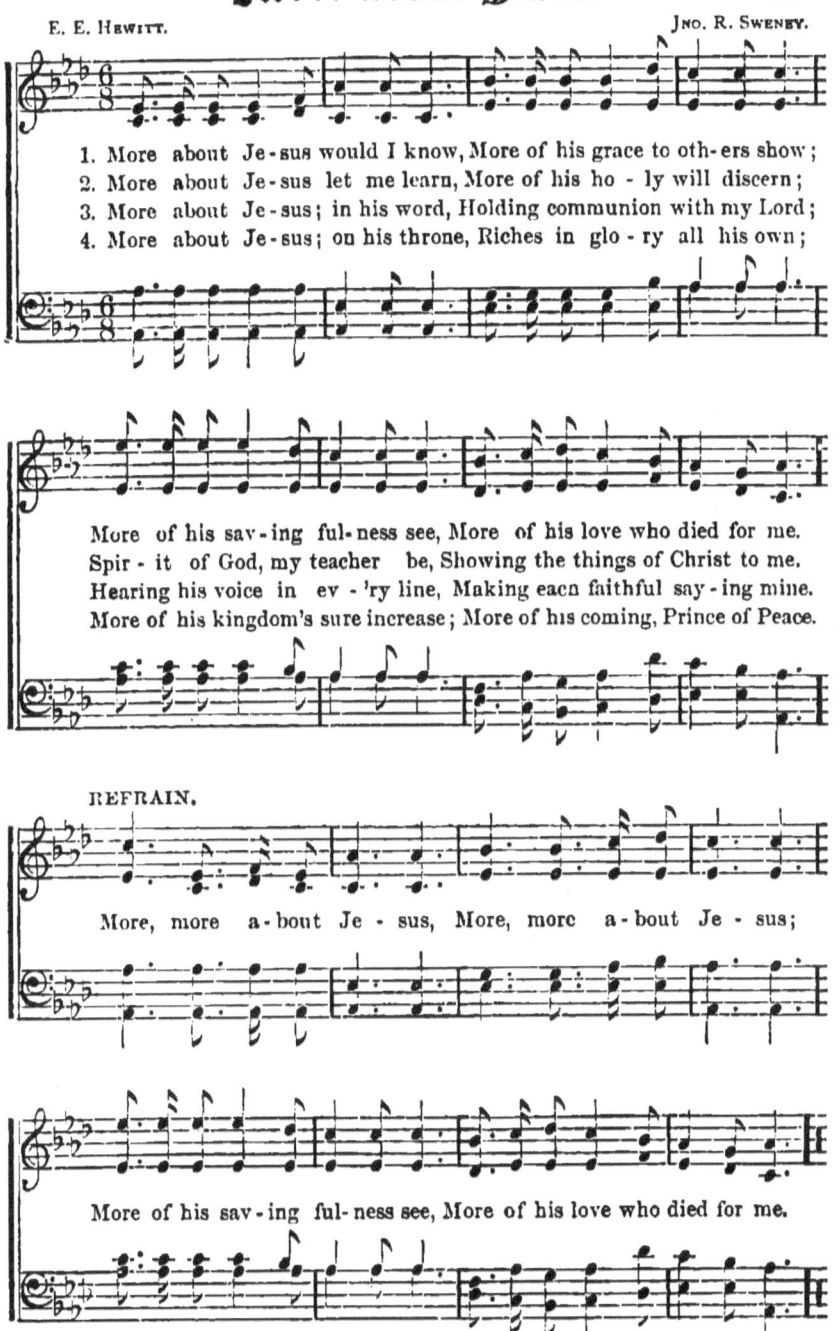

I Love Thy Will.—CONCLUDED. 111

What-e'er thy will, I love it still; A-men, a-men, my Lord.

Kingdom, Power, and Glory.

E. E. HEWITT.   JNO. R. SWENEY.

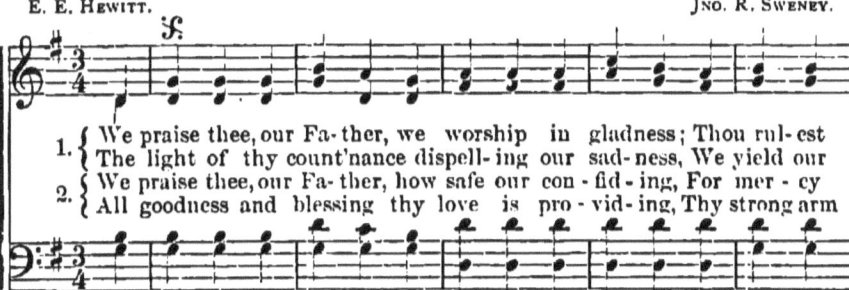

1. We praise thee, our Fa-ther, we worship in gladness; Thou rul-est
   The light of thy count'nance dispell-ing our sad-ness, We yield our
2. We praise thee, our Fa-ther, how safe our con-fid-ing, For mer-cy
   All goodness and blessing thy love is pro-vid-ing, Thy strong arm

D.S.—thine is the kingdom, the power and the glo-ry, For-ev-er

the waves of the sea;   al-legiance to thee.   For thine is the kingdom, the
upholdeth thy throne;   defending thine own.

and ev-er, a-men.

power, and the glo-ry, For-ev-er and ev-er, for-ev-er, a-men; For

3 We praise thee, our Father, we bless and adore thee,
   With bright, gleaming hosts of the sky;
   With reverent spirits we bow down before thee;
   Thy name is exalted most high.

4 We praise thee, our Father, our God everlasting;
   The ages thy glories repeat;
   The saints in thy mansions with rapture are casting
   Their starry-gemmed crowns at thy feet.

Copyright, 1889, by Jno R Sweney.

O Saviour, Stay.—CONCLUDED. 113

stay, go not a-way, But take this heart of mine.
stay, and seal to-day My heart for-ev-er thine.

Saviour, stay,

Draw Me, O Lord.

FANNY J. CROSBY.   WM. J. KIRKPATRICK.

1. { Draw me, O Lord, with the cords of thy love, Draw me still closer to thee; }
   { What is the world to the mansion above Thou art prepar-ing for me? }

2. { Draw me, O Lord, to the arms of thy rest, O-pen to welcome me there; }
   { Soon shall I fly like a bird to its nest, Ev-er thy glo-ry to share. }

CHORUS.

There is my home, my beauti-ful home, Over the wave-girded sea;

There in thy likeness my soul shall awake, Happy, dear Saviour, in thee.
                                                   dear Saviour, in thee.

3 Draw me, O Lord, where the friends of the past
Roam on that bright, sunny plain;
O that my spirit may join them at last,
Never to lose them again.

4 Draw me, O Lord, where the faithful and tried
Labor and sorrow no more;
Draw me away where I hope to abide,
Anchored and safe on the shore.

The Joyful Sound-H   Copyright, 1889, by WM. J. KIRKPATRICK.

Let Us Not Be Weary. 115

E. E. Hewitt.   Jno R. Sweney.

1. Scattering the seed, the precious, precious seed, Seeds of love and faith and duty;
2. Scattering the seed, wherever we may be, Finding there a field of la-bor;

Hear, oh, hear the word, the harvest will appear, Glorious in wealth and beauty.
Sowing seeds of love which, springing up, shall bear Blessing to a needy neighbor.

CHORUS.

Let us not be weary, weary in well-doing,
Praying while we sow the seed that cannot die;

Sowing by all waters, sowing to the Spirit, We shall reap with rapture by and by.

3 Scattering the seed thro' weary, darksome hours,
Long may seem the night of weeping;
But the day will dawn of happy harvest time,
Time of everlasting reaping.

4 Scattering the seed with willing heart and hand,
Joyful is the harvest story;
Bringing home the sheaves, we'll shout the jubilee,
To our Lord be all the glory!

Copyright, 1888, by Jno. R. Sweney.

118. There's a Great Day Coming.

W. L. T.   W. L. Thompson.

1. There's a great day com-ing, A great day com-ing, There's a great day coming by and by, When the saints and the sinners shall be part-ed right and left, Are you read-y for that day to come?

2. There's a bright day com-ing, A bright day com-ing, There's a bright day coming by and by, But its brightness shall on-ly come to them that love the Lord, Are you read-y for that day to come?

3. There's a sad day com-ing, A sad day com-ing, There's a sad day coming by and by, When the sinner shall hear his doom, "De-part, I know ye not," Are you read-y for that day to come?

CHORUS.

Are you read-y? are you read-y? Are you read-y for the judgment day? Are you ready? are you ready For the judgment day?

By permission of W. L. Thompson & Co., East Liverpool, O.

Return.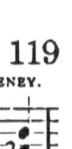

JAMES L. BLACK.   JNO R. SWENEY.

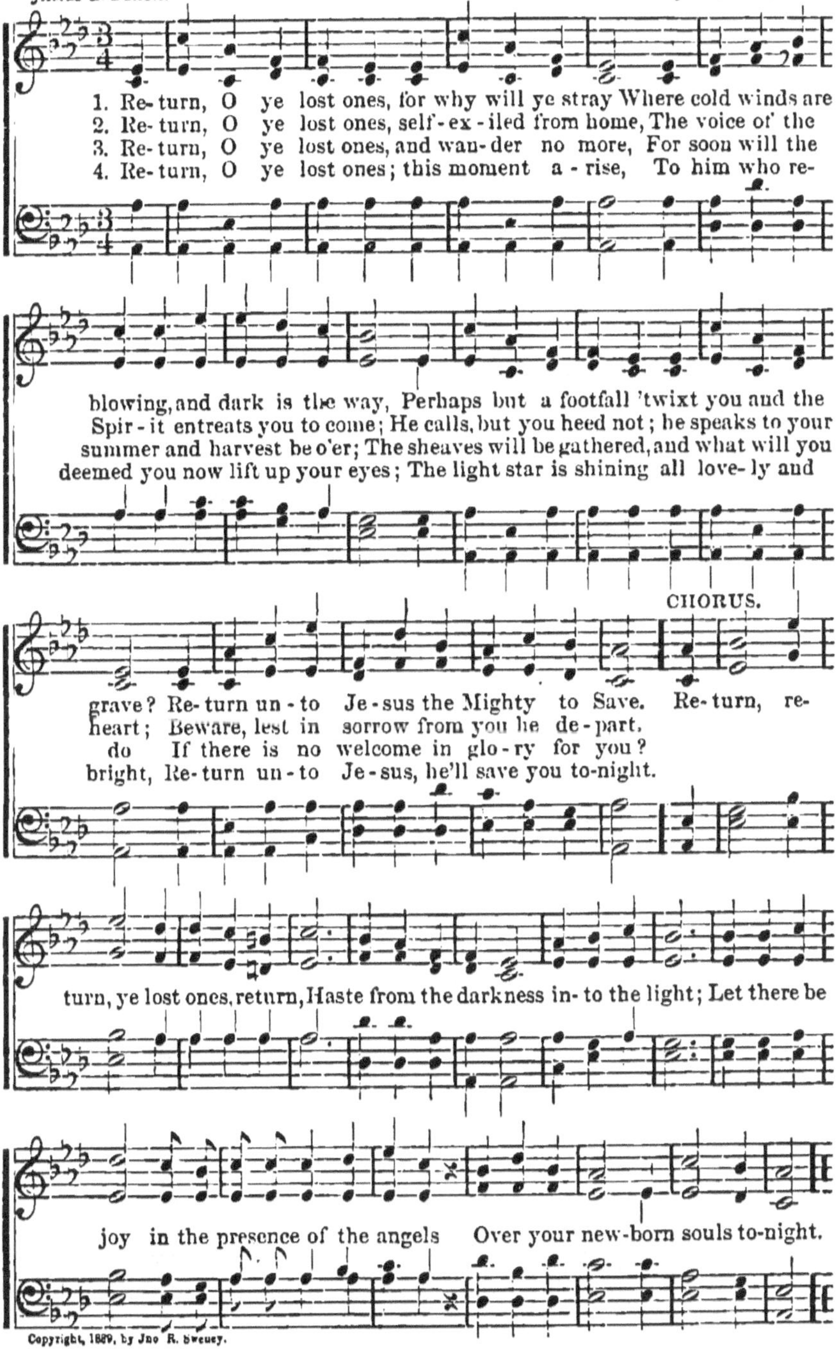

1. Re-turn, O ye lost ones, for why will ye stray Where cold winds are
2. Re-turn, O ye lost ones, self-ex-iled from home, The voice of the
3. Re-turn, O ye lost ones, and wan-der no more, For soon will the
4. Re-turn, O ye lost ones; this moment a-rise, To him who re-

blowing, and dark is the way, Perhaps but a footfall 'twixt you and the
Spir-it entreats you to come; He calls, but you heed not; he speaks to your
summer and harvest be o'er; The sheaves will be gathered, and what will you
deemed you now lift up your eyes; The light star is shining all love-ly and

CHORUS.

grave? Re-turn un-to Je-sus the Mighty to Save. Re-turn, re-
heart; Beware, lest in sorrow from you he de-part.
do If there is no welcome in glo-ry for you?
bright, Re-turn un-to Je-sus, he'll save you to-night.

turn, ye lost ones, return, Haste from the darkness in-to the light; Let there be

joy in the presence of the angels Over your new-born souls to-night.

Copyright, 1879, by Jno R. Sweney.

122 Open Thou Mine Eyes.

E. E. Hewitt.   Jno. R. Sweney.

1. Wait-ing by the way-side For the coming Mas-ter, List'ning for his footsteps drawing nigh; All is dark and dreary, Waiting, sad and weary, Help me, Jesus, Master; hear, oh, hear my cry.
2. Wait-ing now no long-er, Faith is growing stronger, With the gracious Master standing near; What is this glad greeting? Hasten to the meeting! Mer-cy now is streaming from the sunlit skies.
3. In my sin and sor-row Cour-age I will bor-row From this sweet old sto-ry of his grace; Looking on my Saviour, Trusting in his fav-or, Now my eyes, long darkened, see his smiling face.

CHORUS.

Open thou mine eyes, Open thou mine eyes, To thy rays of healing streaming from the skies; Open thou mine eyes, Mer-cy now is streaming from the sunlit skies.

Copyright, 1889, by Jno. R. Sweney.

Healing at the Fountain. 123

Fanny J. Crosby. Wm. J. Kirkpatrick.

1. There is healing at the fount-ain, Come, behold the crimson tide,
2. There is healing at the fount-ain, Come and find it, wea-ry soul,
3. There is healing at the fount-ain, Look to Je-sus now and live,
4. There is healing at the fount-ain, Precious fountain filled with blood,

Flowing down from Calvary's mountain, Where the Prince of Glory died.
There your sins may all be cov-ered; Je-sus waits to make you whole.
At the cross lay down your bur-den; All your wanderings he'll forgive,
Come, O come, the Saviour calls you; Come and plunge beneath its flood.

CHORUS.

O the fountain! blessed, healing fountain! I am glad 'tis flowing free,

O the fountain! precious, cleansing fountain! Praise the Lord, it cleanseth me.

Copyright, 1885, by Wm. J. Kirkpatrick.

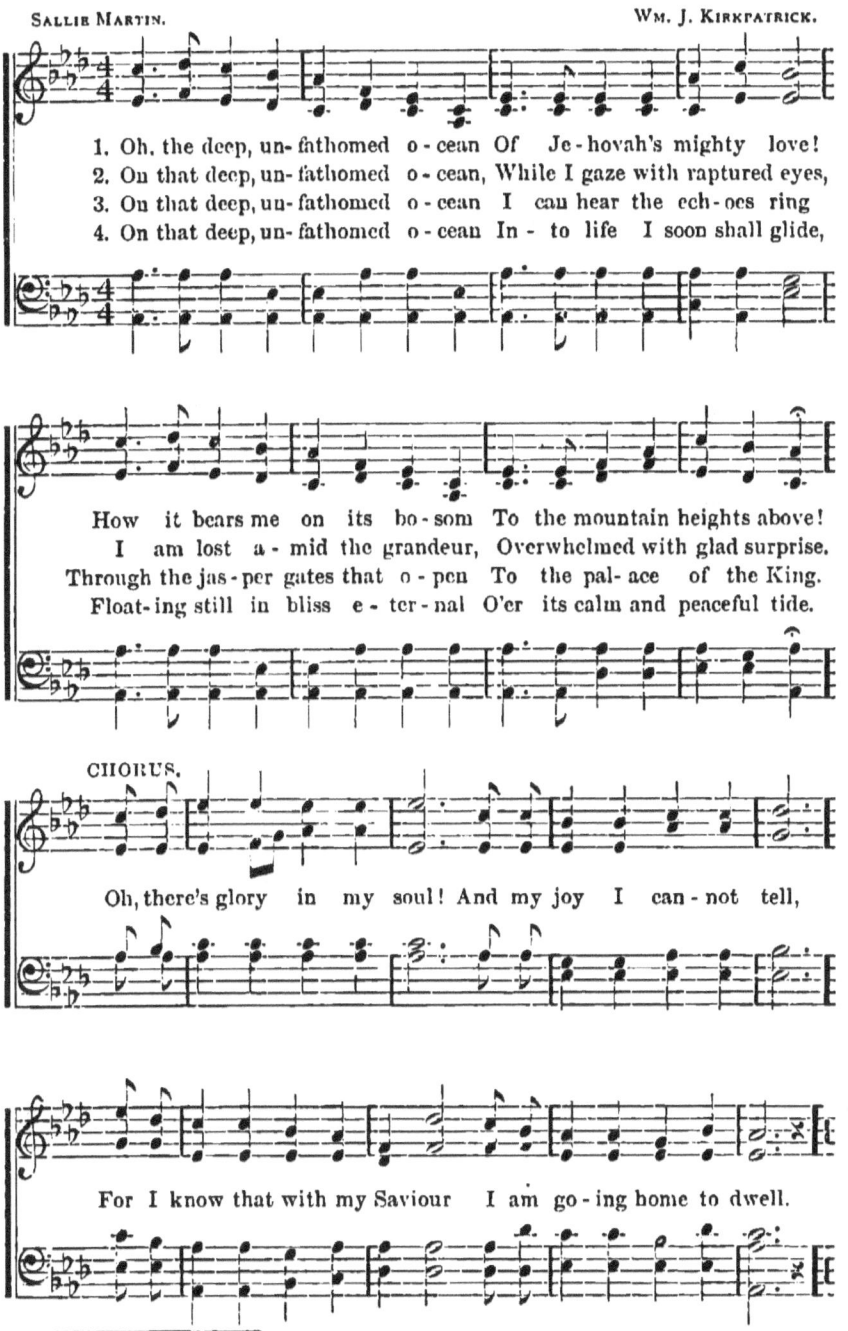

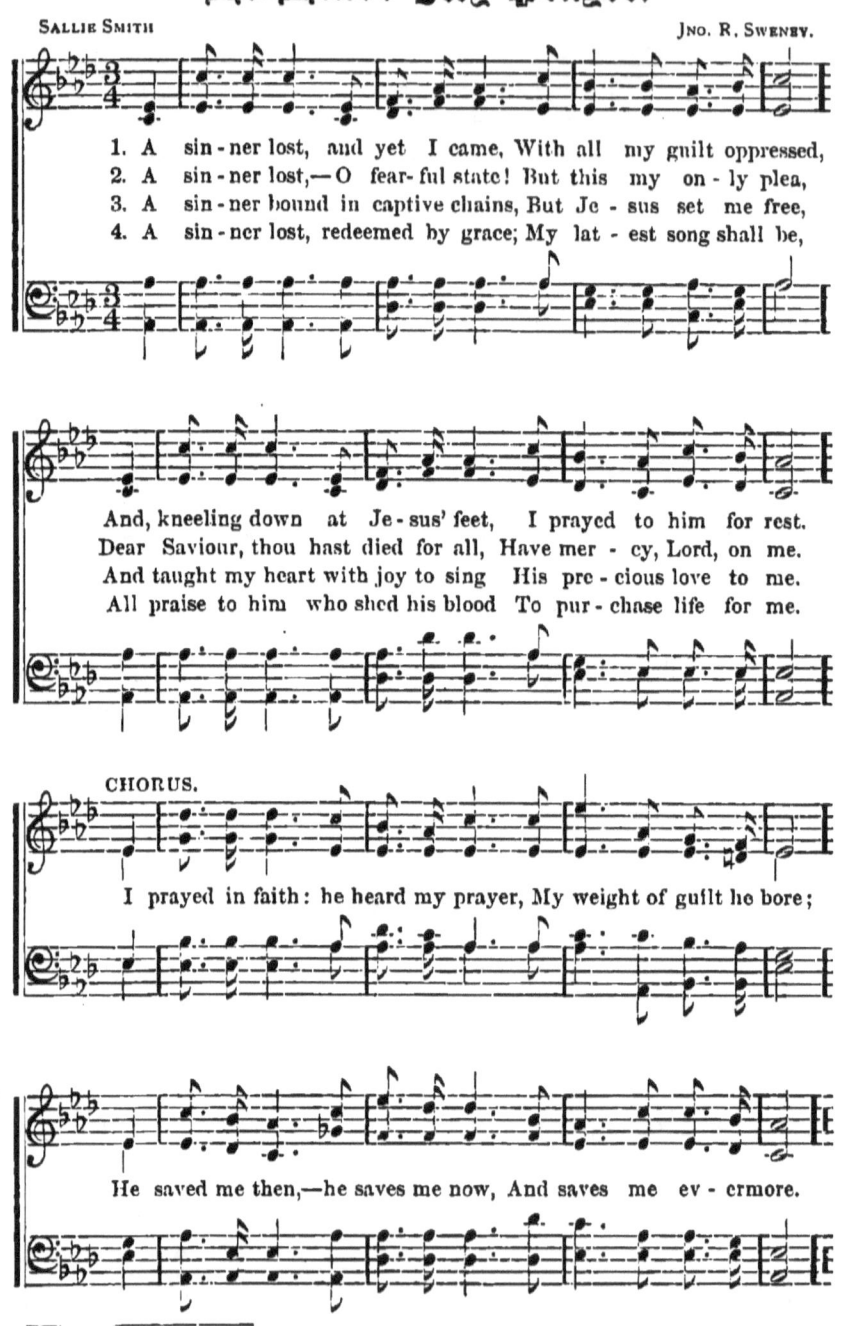

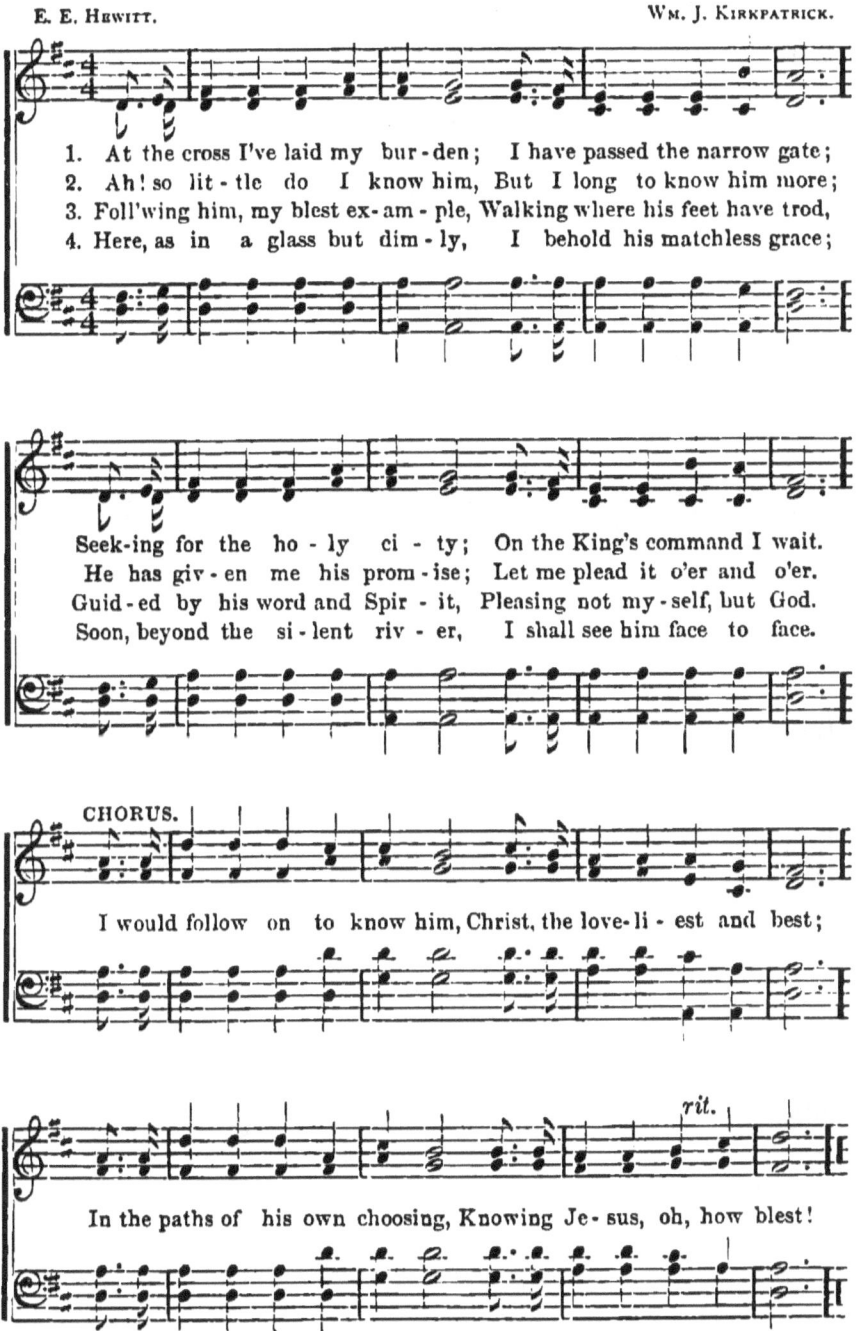

132. Marching On to Victory.

NATHAN DUN, D.D.   TEMPERANCE SONG.   WM. J. KIRKPATRICK.

1. The temperance cause is moving on, Our State and nation shall be free;
2. Thy kingdom come, O Lord, we pray; 'Tis coming soon, the world shall see;
3. The temperance banner soon shall wave From north to south, from sea to sea:

A better day begins to dawn: We're marching on to victo-ry!
God save our homes, we cry to-day, While marching on to victo-ry.
With earnest step, ye true and brave, We're marching on to victo-ry!

CHORUS.

We're marching on, ... we're marching on, ... We're marching on ... to vic-to-ry; .... A better day ... begins to dawn, ... We are marching, marching on to victory.

We're marching on to vic-to-ry, to vic-to-ry, on to vic-to-ry. to vic-to-ry.

4 We soon shall join the glad refrain:
"The land we love at last is free!
Hosanna! swell the joyful strain!"
We're marching on to victory!

5 The crowning work will soon be done:
God speed the coming jubilee!
Behold, the day is almost won!
We're marching on to victory!

Copyright, 1889, by Wm. J. Kirkpatrick.

Victory is Near.—CONCLUDED. 135

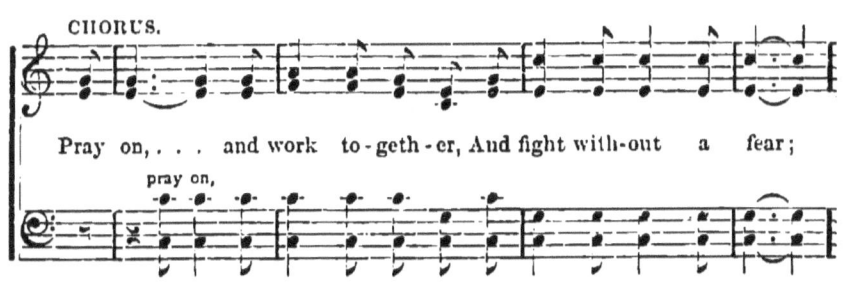

Awake, Awake.—CONTINUED. 139

His blessings fall around us Like dew and summer showers,

He cheers the path before us, And makes it bright with flowers,

D.C.

He cheers the path before us, And makes it bright with flowers.

SOLO.

He is watching kind-ly o'er us, Bending low our song to hear,

And we know with ev'-ry mo-ment Guardian an-gels hov-er near,

142. Companionship with Jesus.

MARY D. JAMES.   WM. J. KIRKPATRICK.

1. Oh, bless-ed fel-low-ship divine! Oh, joy supremely sweet! Com-pan-ion-ship with Je-sus here Makes life with bliss re-plete. In un-ion with the pur-est one I find my heav'n on earth be-gun.
2. I'm walking close to Je-sus' side, So close that I can hear The soft-est wisp-ers of his love, In fel-low-ship so dear, And feel his great, al-might-y hand Protects me in this hos-tile land.
3. I'm lean-ing on his lov-ing breast, Along life's weary way; My path, il-lumined by his smiles, Grows brighter day by day. No foes, no woes my heart can fear, With my al-might-y Friend so near.
4. I know his shelt'ring wings of love Are always o'er me spread, And tho' the storms may fiercely rage, All calm and free from dread, My peace-ful spir-it ev-er sings, "I'll trust the cov-ert of thy wings."

CHORUS.

Oh, wondrous bliss! oh, joy sublime! I've Je-sus with me all the time.

Oh, wondrous bliss! oh, joy sublime! I've Je-sus with me all the time.

Copyright, 1875, by WM. J. KIRKPATRICK.

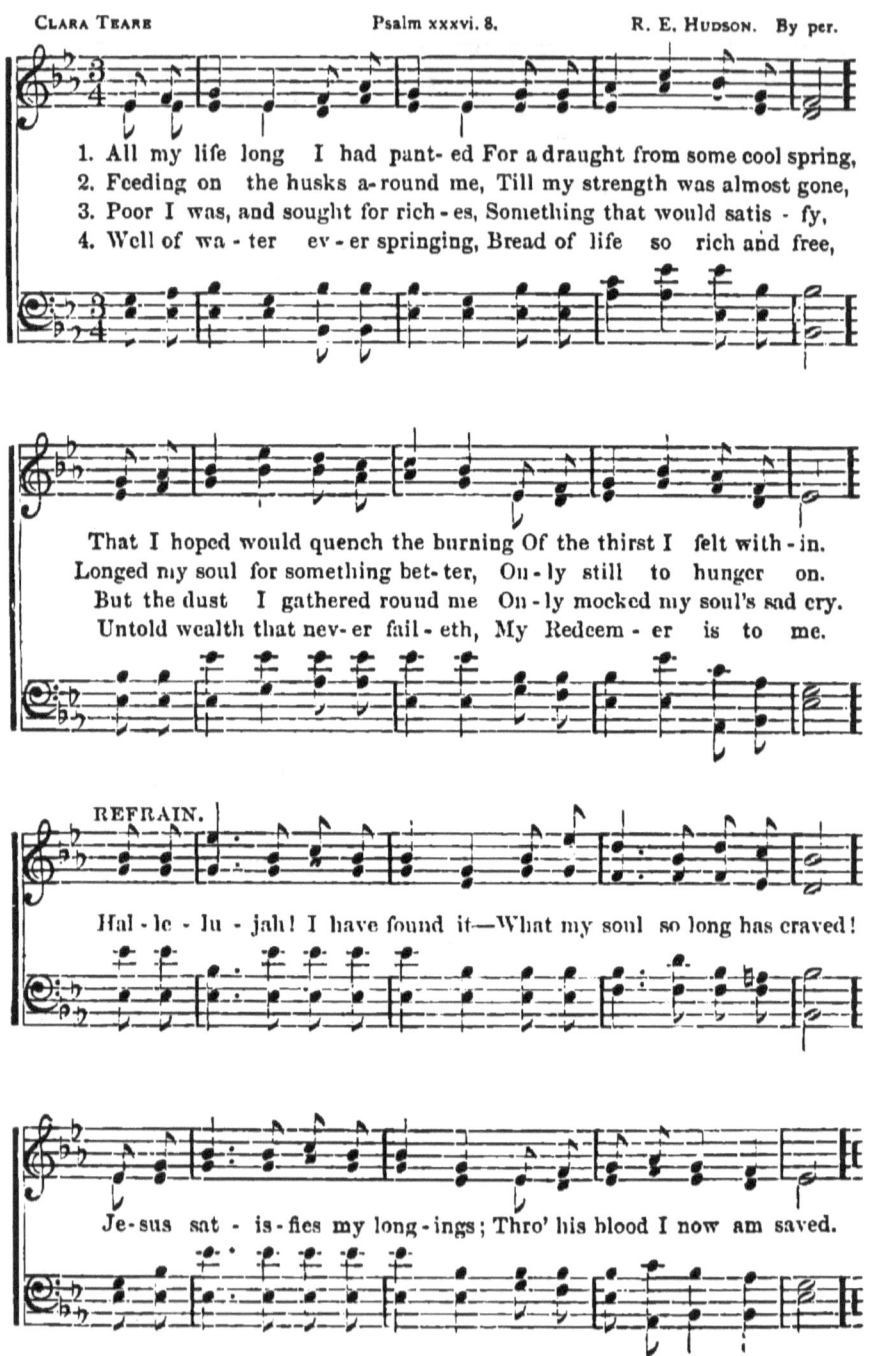

146. Only Believe.

Emma M. Johnston. — Mark v. 36. — Wm. J. Kirkpatrick.

1. Oh, why should we wres-tle with fears And doubts, which the Spir-it must grieve? And why should we languish in sor-row and tears, When there's nothing to do but be-lieve.
2. His word is as-sur-ance com-plete; Thy sins and thine i-dols now leave; Come, pleading his promise, and fall at his feet, Then you've nothing to do but be-lieve.
3. How ea-sy the terms of his grace: 'Tis on-ly to ask and re-ceive; The seal of his fav-or, the smile of his face, Are for those who will on-ly be-lieve.

CHORUS.

Be-lieve, be-lieve, be-lieve, On-ly on Je-sus be-lieve; Sal-va-tion is wait-ing for you and for me, There is nothing to do but be-lieve.

Copyright, 1889, by Wm. J. Kirkpatrick.

The Pleading Saviour. 147

Rev. John Love, Jr. J. J. Lowe.

1. Jesus calls thee, wand'rer, come; Calls to-day, calls to-day; Longs to bid thee welcome
2. Patiently he waits for thee, Waits to-day, waits to-day, Offers full sal- vation
3. He will cleanse your sins away, All away, all away; Why delay the glorious
4. Now he pleads with tender voice, Pleads to-day, pleads to-day, Make his love your
[sacred

home, Home to-day, home to-day; Wondrous love his heart doth feel, Wondrous
free, Free to-day, free to-day; Wouldst thou know his saving grace? Wouldst thou
day? Why de-lay? why de-lay? Oh, the joy you might receive If on
choice, Choose to-day, choose to-day; Shall his pleading be refused? Shall his

Fine.

love he would reveal, For his own thy life would seal, Seal to-day, seal to-day.
feel his strong embrace, Thro' thy life his favor trace? Yield to-day, yield to-day.
him you would believe, Thought nor fancy can conceive: Don't delay, don't delay.
mer-cy be abused? Come, by grace divine enthused, Come to-day, come to-day.

D. S.—I will cleanse thy sins away; Why delay? why delay?

REFRAIN. D. S.

Come to-day,   come to- day,   Hear the bless - - ed Saviour say:
  Come to-day,   come to-day,   Hear the blessed

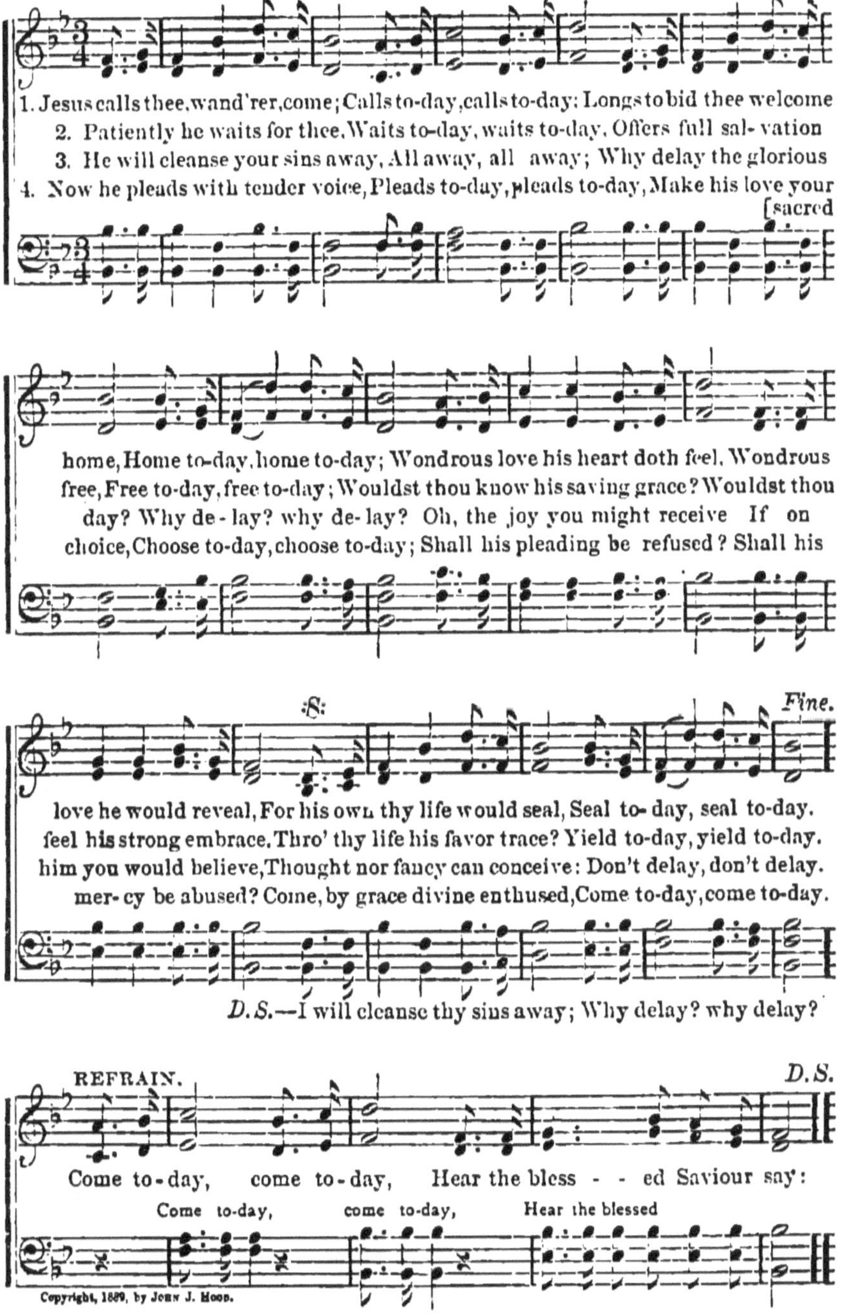

Copyright, 1889, by John J. Hood.

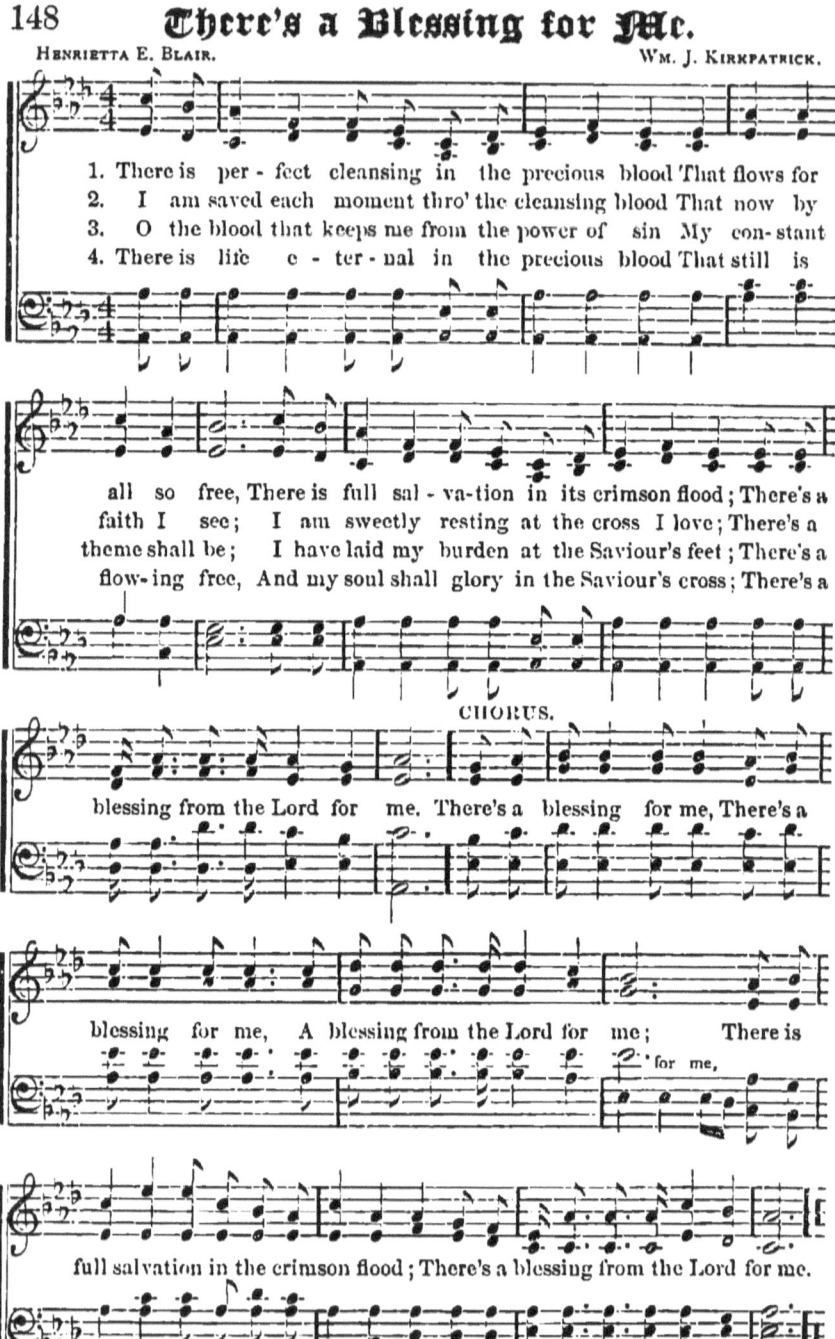

149. My Heart's Dear Home.

Fanny J. Crosby. — Wm. J. Kirkpatrick.

1. When lost among the wild, dark mountains, Far, far from thee, I heard thy gentle
2. When lost among the wild, dark mountains, Sad was my cry, Till softly came the
3. O teach me to adore and praise thee, Saviour divine; Now I have made a
4. Wherever thou wilt lead, I'll follow Close, close to thee; One prayer alone my

voice, my Saviour, Calling in love to me.
words so tender, "Fear not, for here am I."
full sur-render, All that I am is thine.
soul is breathing, Saviour, abide with me.

CHORUS.

Safe within thy arms of mercy, Nev-er more to roam; O, let me rest in

D.S.—peace forev-er, Safe in my heart's dear home.

Copyright, 1888, by Wm. J. Kirkpatrick.

150. Jesus Sought Me.

Tune above.

1 Long, weary years in sin I wandered,
  Far from the fold:
Till Christ, the loving Shepherd, found me.
  Out in the midnight cold.
Hungry and thirsty then he led me
  Where waters flow,
And with refreshing manna fed me,
  He washed me white as snow.

Cho.—Vain, delusive world, forever,
  Now I sing farewell,
Jesus, my loving Saviour, keeps me,
  His love I'll gladly tell.

2 O for a heart to praise my Saviour!
  For he has died,
And my exulting soul finds favor
  Close to his bleeding side;
There may I cling through life, and never
  Grieve him away,
And in those heavenly mansions ever
  Spend an eternal day.

3 Salvation thrills my soul with gladness,
  Praise ye the Lord!
No more I'll yield again to sadness,
  But trust in the blessed Word.
To Father, Son, and Holy Spirit,
  All three in one,
Be glory through a Saviour's merit,
  Ever thy will be done.

—Dr. H. L. Gilmour.

151. When all Thy Mercies.

JOSEPH ADDISON.
Tune, MANOAH. C.M.

1. When all thy mer-cies, O my God, My ris-ing soul sur-veys,
2. Through hidden dangers, toils, and deaths, It gently cleared my way;

Transport-ed with the view, I'm lost In won-der, love, and praise.
And through the pleasing snares of vice, More to be feared than they.

3 Through every period of my life
   Thy goodness I'll pursue;
   And after death, in distant worlds,
   The pleasing theme renew.

4 Through all eternity to thee
   A grateful song I'll raise;
   But oh, eternity's too short
   To utter all thy praise.

152. How Sweet the Name.

JOHN NEWTON.
Tune, DOWNS. C.M.

1. How sweet the name of Je-sus sounds In a be-liev-er's ear!

It soothes his sor-rows, heals his wounds, And drives away his fear.

2 It makes the wounded spirit whole,
   And calms the troubled breast;
   'Tis manna to the hungry soul,
   And to the weary, rest.

3 Dear name! the rock on which I build,
   My shield and hiding-place;
   My never-failing treasure, filled
   With boundless stores of grace!

4 Jesus, my Shepherd, Saviour, Friend,
   My Prophet, Priest, and King,
   My Lord, my Life, my Way, my End,
   Accept the praise I bring!

5 I would thy boundless love proclaim
   With every fleeting breath;
   So shall the music of thy name
   Refresh my soul in death.

153 Watchman, Tell us of the Night.

Sir John Bowring.   Tune, WATCHMAN. 7s, d.

1. Watchman, tell us of the night, What its signs of promise are;
Traveler, o'er yon mountain's height See that glo-ry-beam-ing star!
Watchman, does its beauteous ray Aught of hope or joy for-tell?
Traveler, yes; it brings the day, Prom-ised day of Is-ra-el.

2 Watchman, tell us of the night;
Higher yet that star ascends.
Traveler, blessedness and light,
Peace and truth, its course portends!
Watchman, will its beams alone
Gild the spot that gave them birth?
Traveler, ages are its own,
See, it bursts o'er all the earth!

3 Watchman, tell us of the night,
For the morning seems to dawn.
Traveler, darkness takes its flight;
Doubt and terror are withdrawn.
Watchman, let thy wandering cease;
Hie thee to thy quiet home!
Traveler, lo! the Prince of Peace,
Lo! the Son of God is come!

---

154   The Lord's my Shepherd.   Tune, DOWNS.

1 The Lord's my Shepherd, I'll not want;
He makes me down to lie
In pastures green; he leadeth me
The quiet waters by.

2 My soul he doth restore again,
And me to walk doth make
Within the paths of righteousness,
E'en for his own name's sake.

3 Yea, though I walk through death's
Yet will I fear no ill,   [dark vale,

For thou art with me, and thy rod
And staff me comfort still.

4 A table thou hast furnished me
In presence of my foes;
My head thou dost with oil anoint,
And my cup overflows.

5 Goodness and mercy all my life
Shall surely follow me,
And in God's house forevermore
My dwelling-place shall be.

155. Go, Labor On.

H. Bonar. Tune, MISSIONARY CHANT. L. M.

1. Go, la-bor on; spend and be spent, Thy joy to do the Father's will;
It is the way the Master went; Should not the servant tread it still?

2 Go, labor on; 'tis not for naught;
  Thine earthly loss is heavenly gain;
  Men heed thee, love thee, praise thee not;
  The Master praises,—what are men?

3 Go, labor on; your hands are weak;
  Your knees are faint, your soul cast down;
  Yet falter not; the prize you seek
  Is near,—a kingdom and a crown!

4 Toil on, faint not; keep watch, and pray!
  Be wise the erring soul to win;
  Go forth into the world's highway;
  Compel the wanderer to come in.

5 Toil on, and in thy toil rejoice;
  For toil comes rest, for exile home;
  Soon shalt thou hear the Bridegroom's voice,
  The midnight peal, "Behold, I come!"

156. Awake, my Soul.

P. Doddridge. Tune, CHRISTMAS. C. M.

1. A-wake, my soul, stretch ev'ry nerve, And press with vigor on; A heavenly race demands thy zeal, And an immortal crown, And an immortal crown.

2 A cloud of witnesses around
  Hold thee in full survey;
  Forget the steps already trod,
  And onward urge thy way.

3 'Tis God's all-animating voice
  That calls thee from on high;
  'Tis his own hand presents the prize
  To thine aspiring eye:—

4 That prize, with peerless glories bright,
  Which shall new luster boast,
  When victors' wreaths and monarchs' gems
  Shall blend in common dust.

5 Blest Saviour, introduced by thee,
  Have I my race begun;
  And, crowned with victory, at thy feet
  I'll lay my honors down.

157. Eternal Beam of Light.

C. WESLEY. Tune, LOUVAN. L. M.

1. E-ter-nal Beam of light divine, Fountain of un-exhaust-ed love,
2. Je-sus, the wea-ry wanderer's rest, Give me thy ea-sy yoke to bear;

In whom the Father's glories shine, Thro' earth beneath, and heaven above;
With steadfast patience arm my breast, With spotless love and low-ly fear.

3 Thankful I take the cup from thee,
   Prepared and mingled by thy skill;
   Though bitter to the taste it be,
   Powerful the wounded soul to heal.
4 Be thou, O Rock of Ages, nigh! [gone,
   So shall each murmuring thought be
   And grief, and fear, and care shall fly,
   As clouds before the midday sun.

5 Speak to my warring passions, "Peace;"
   Say to my trembling heart, "Be still;"
   Thy power my strength and fortress is,
   For all things serve thy sovereign will.
6 O Death! where is thy sting? where
   Thy boasted victory, O Grave? [now
   Who shall contend with God? or who
   Can hurt whom God delights to save?

158. Blest be the Tie that Binds.

JOHN FAWCETT. Tune, DENNIS. S. M.

1. Blest be the tie that binds Our hearts in Chris-tian love; The
2. Be-fore our Fa-ther's throne We pour our ar-dent prayers; Our

fel-low-ship of kind-red minds Is like to that a-bove.
fears, our hopes, our aims are one, Our com-forts and our cares.

3 We share our mutual woes,
   Our mutual burdens bear;
   And often for each other flows
   The sympathizing tear.

4 When we asunder part,
   It gives us inward pain;
   But we shall still be joined in heart,
   And hope to meet again.

159. Full Salvation.

F. H. STEELE. E. E. NICKERSON.

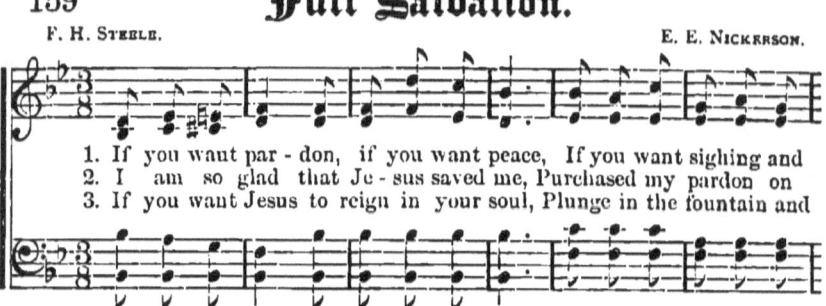

1. If you want par-don, if you want peace, If you want sighing and
2. I am so glad that Je-sus saved me, Purchased my pardon on
3. If you want Jesus to reign in your soul, Plunge in the fountain and

CHO.—Liv-ing be-neath the shade of the cross, Counting the jew-els of

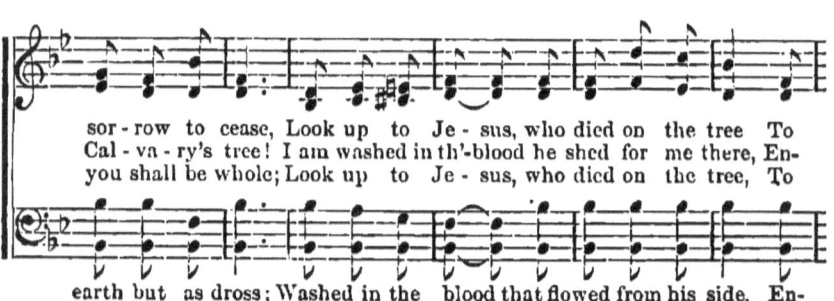

sor-row to cease, Look up to Je-sus, who died on the tree To
Cal-va-ry's tree! I am washed in th'-blood he shed for me there, En-
you shall be whole; Look up to Je-sus, who died on the tree, To

earth but as dross; Washed in the blood that flowed from his side, En-

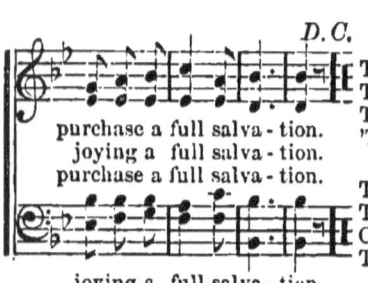

D.C.

purchase a full salva-tion.
joying a full salva-tion.
purchase a full salva-tion.

joying a full salva-tion.

4
There's peace in believing, sweet peace to the soul,
To know that he maketh me perfectly whole;
There's joy everlasting to feel his blood flow,
'Tis life my Redeemer to know.

5
There's peace in believing, sweet peace to the soul,
To know that he maketh me perfectly whole;
Oh, come to the fountain, oh, come at his call,
There's healing and cleansing for all.

From "Highway Songs," by per.

160. Take All My Sins Away.

M. B. MARECHALE BOOTH.

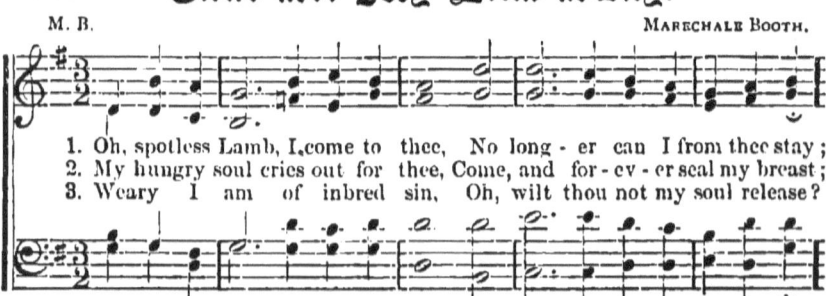

1. Oh, spotless Lamb, I come to thee, No long-er can I from thee stay;
2. My hungry soul cries out for thee, Come, and for-ev-er seal my breast;
3. Weary I am of inbred sin, Oh, wilt thou not my soul release?

Take All My Sins Away.—CONCLUDED.

Break ev-'ry chain, now set me free, Take all my sins a-way.
To thy dear arms at last I flee, There on-ly can I rest.
En-ter, and speak me pure with-in, Give me thy per-fect peace.

D.S.—My precious Sav-iour, full of love, Take all my sins a-way.

Take all my sins a-way, Take all my sins a-way,

161. Come, My Soul.

JOHN NEWTON.   Tune, SEYMOUR. 7s.

1. Come, my soul, thy suit pre-pare, Je-sus loves to answer prayer;
2. Lord, I come to thee for rest; Take pos-ses-sion of my breast;
3. While I am a pil-grim here, Let thy love my spir-it cheer;
4. Show me what I have to do; Ev-'ry hour my strength renew;

He him-self in-vites thee near, Bids thee ask him, waits to hear.
There thy blood-bought right maintain, And without a riv-al reign.
As my guide, my guard, my friend, Lead me to my journey's end.
Let me live a life of faith, Let me die thy people's death.

162. Must Jesus Bear the Cross.

THOMAS SHEPHERD. Alt.   Tune, MAITLAND. C. M.

1. Must Jesus bear the cross alone, And all the world go free? No, there's a cross for ev-'ry one, And there's a cross for me.

2 How happy are the saints above,
Who once went sorrowing here!
But now they taste unmingled love,
And joy without a tear.

3 The consecrated cross I'll bear,
Till death shall set me free;
And then go home my crown to wear,
For there's a crown for me.

163. Blow ye the Trumpet.

C. WESLEY.   Tune, LISCHER. H. M.

1. Blow ye the trumpet, blow; The gladly solemn sound
Let all the nations know, To earth's remotest bound: The year of jubilee is come:

2. Jesus, our great High Priest, Hath full atonement made:
Ye weary spirits, rest; Ye mournful souls, be glad: The year, etc.

Return, ye ransomed sinners, home, Return, ye ransomed sinners, home.

3 Extol the Lamb of God,
The all-atoning Lamb;
Redemption in his blood
Throughout the world proclaim.

4 Ye slaves of sin and hell,
Your liberty receive,
And safe in Jesus dwell,
And blest in Jesus live.

5 Ye who have sold for naught
Your heritage above,
Shall have it back unbought,
The gift of Jesus' love.

6 The gospel trumpet hear,
The news of heavenly grace,
And saved from earth, appear
Before your Saviour's face.

164 C. Wesley.   **O Glorious Hope.**   Tune, WILLOUGHBY. C.P.M.

1. O glorious hope of perfect love! It lifts me up to things above: It bears on eagles' wings;
It gives my ravished soul a taste, And makes me for some moments feast With Jesus' priests and kings.

2 Rejoicing now in earnest hope,
I stand, and from the mountain top
  See all the land below:
Rivers of milk and honey rise,
And all the fruits of paradise
  In endless plenty grow.

3 A land of corn, and wine, and oil,
Favored with God's peculiar smile,
  With every blessing blest;
There dwells the Lord our Righteous-
And keeps his own in perfect peace, [ness,
  And everlasting rest.

4 O that I might at once go up;
No more on this side Jordan stop,
  But now the land possess;
This moment end my legal years,
Sorrows and sins, and doubts and fears,
  A howling wilderness!

165   **Come on, my Partners.**

1 Come on, my partners in distress,
My comrades through the wilderness,
  Who still your bodies feel;
Awhile forget your griefs and fears,
And look beyond this vale of tears,
  To that celestial hill.

2 Beyond the bounds of time and space,
Look forward to that heavenly place,
  The saints' secure abode;
On faith's strong eagle pinions rise,
And force your passage to the skies,
  And scale the mount of God.

3 Who suffer with our Master here,
We shall before his face appear
  And by his side sit down;
To patient faith the prize is sure,
And all that to the end endure
  The cross, shall wear the crown.

4 Thrice blessed, bliss-inspiring hope!
It lifts the fainting spirits up,
  It brings to life the dead;
Our conflicts here shall soon be past,
And you and I ascend at last,
  Triumphant with our Head.

5 That great mysterious Deity
We soon with open face shall see;
  The beatific sight [praise,
Shall fill the heavenly courts with
And wide diffuse the golden blaze
  Of everlasting light.   —C. Wesley.

166   Welcome, Delightful Morn.   *Tune opposite.*

1 Welcome, delightful morn,
  Thou day of sacred rest,
We hail thy kind return,
  Lord, make these moments blest;
From the low train of mortal toys
We soar to reach immortal joys.

2 Now may the King descend
  And fill his throne of grace;

Thy sceptre, Lord, extend,
  While saints address thy face:
Let sinners feel thy quickening word,
And learn to know and fear the Lord.

3 Descend, celestial Dove!
  With all thy quickening powers,
Disclose a Saviour's love,
  And bless these sacred hours;
Then shall our souls new life obtain,
Nor Sabbaths be bestowed in vain.

167. Look and Believe.

PRISCILLA J. OWENS. WM. J. KIRKPATRICK.

1. The Christ is found, we've waited long, The Holy One, the Promised One;
2. The Man of Grief shall dry thy tears, His hands were bound to set thee free,
3. He calms the storm to give thee peace, He dies thine endless life to be,

Our fears are gone, our hopes are strong In God's vic-to-rious Son.
His blood shall cleanse the sin of years, Come, trembling heart, and see.
He lives to bid thy sor-row cease, Now come to him and see.

CHORUS.

Oh, look and believe, oh, come and receive The Christ who died for thee;
The Son of Man is the Son of God; Come, doubting heart, and see.

Copyright, 1889, by Wm. J. Kirkpatrick.

168. Just as thou art.

1 Just as thou art, without one trace
  Of love, or joy, or inward grace,
  Or meetness for the heavenly place,
    O guilty sinner, come.

2 Burdened with guilt, wouldst thou be blest?
  Trust not the world; it gives no rest;
  Christ brings relief to hearts opprest—
    O weary sinner, come.

3 Come, leave thy burden at the cross;
  Count all thy gains but empty dross;
  His grace o'erpays all earthly loss—
    O needy sinner, come.

4 Come, hither bring thy boding fears,
  Thy aching heart, thy bursting tears;
  'Tis mercy's voice salutes thine ears;
    O trembling sinner, come.

5 "The Spirit and the Bride say, Come;"
  Rejoicing saints re-echo, Come;
  Who thirsts, who faints, who will, may come;
    Thy Saviour calls thee, come!

169. There is a Fountain.

COWPER. Arranged by W. J. K.

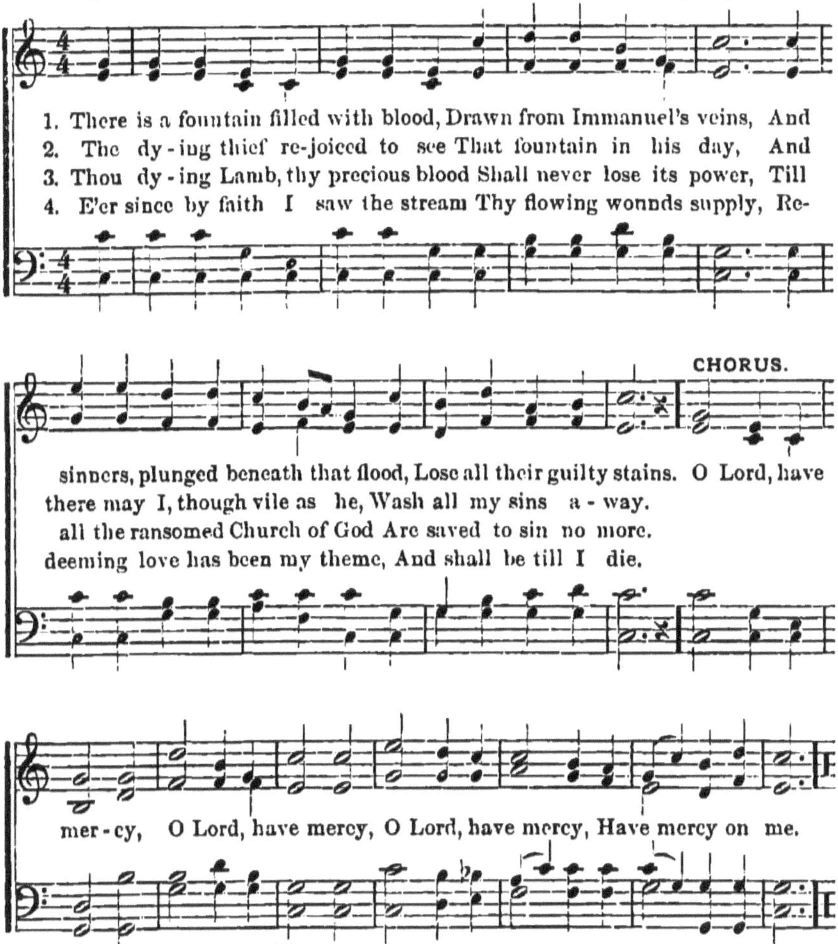

1. There is a fountain filled with blood, Drawn from Immanuel's veins, And sinners, plunged beneath that flood, Lose all their guilty stains. O Lord, have mercy, O Lord, have mercy, O Lord, have mercy, Have mercy on me.
2. The dying thief rejoiced to see That fountain in his day, And there may I, though vile as he, Wash all my sins away.
3. Thou dying Lamb, thy precious blood Shall never lose its power, Till all the ransomed Church of God Are saved to sin no more.
4. E'er since by faith I saw the stream Thy flowing wounds supply, Redeeming love has been my theme, And shall be till I die.

Copyright, 1889, by Wm. J. Kirkpatrick.

170. Alas! and did.

1 Alas! and did my Saviour bleed?
And did my Sovereign die?
Would he devote that sacred head
For such a worm as I?

2 Was it for crimes that I have done,
He groaned upon the tree?
Amazing pity! grace unknown!
And love beyond degree!

3 Well might the sun in darkness hide,
And shut his glories in,
When Christ, the mighty Maker, died,
For man, the creature's sin.

4 Thus might I hide my blushing face
While his dear cross appears;
Dissolve my heart in thankfulness,
And melt mine eyes to tears.

5 But drops of grief can ne'er repay
The debt of love I owe:
Here, Lord, I give myself away,—
'Tis all that I can do.   —I. WATTS.

171. How do Thy Mercies.

C. Wesley.
Tune, FEDERAL STREET. L. M.

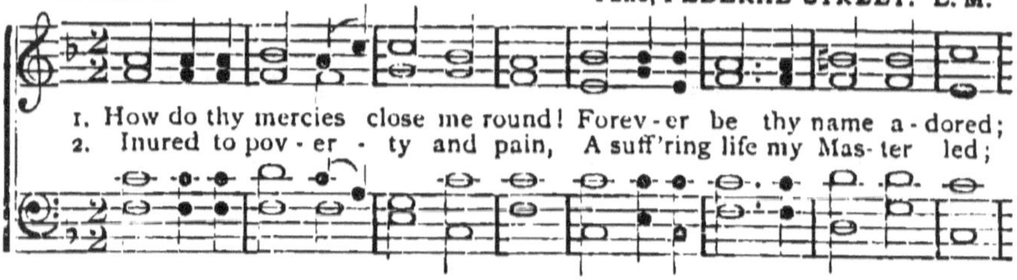

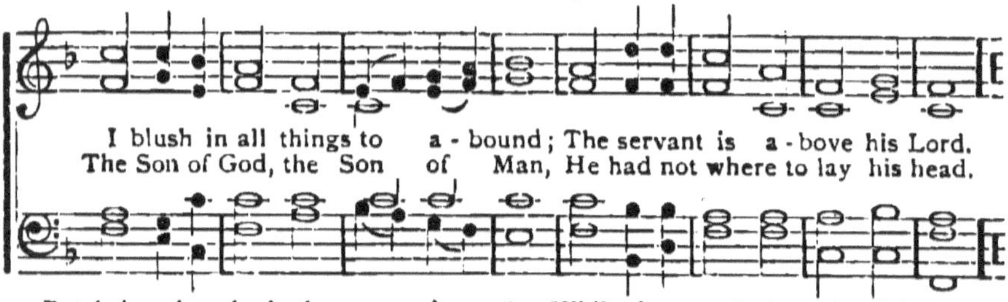

1. How do thy mercies close me round! Forev-er be thy name a-dored;
   I blush in all things to a-bound; The servant is a-bove his Lord.
2. Inured to pov-er-ty and pain, A suff'ring life my Mas-ter led;
   The Son of God, the Son of Man, He had not where to lay his head.

3 But lo! a place he hath prepared
   For me, whom watchful angels keep;
   Yea, he himself becomes my guard;
   He smooths my bed, and gives me sleep.

4 Jesus protects; my fears, be gone;
   What can the Rock of Ages move?
   Safe in thy arms I lay me down,
   Thine everlasting arms of love.

5 While thou art intimately nigh,
   Who, who shall violate my rest?
   Sin, earth, and hell I now defy:
   I lean upon my Saviour's breast.

6 I rest beneath the Almighty's shade;
   My griefs expire, my troubles cease;
   Thou, Lord, on whom my soul is stayed,
   Wilt keep me still in perfect peace.

172. Depth of Mercy!

C. Wesley.
Tune, PLEYEL'S HYMN. 7s.

1. Depth of mer-cy! can there be Mer-cy still reserved for me?
   Can my God his wrath for-bear,— Me, the chief of sin-ners, spare?

2 I have long withstood his grace;
   Long provoked him to his face;
   Would not hearken to his calls;
   Grieved him by a thousand falls.

3 Now incline me to repent;
   Let me now my sins lament;
   Now my foul revolt deplore,
   Weep, believe, and sin no more.

4 Kindled his relentings are;
   Me he now delights to spare;
   Cries, "How shall I give thee up?"
   Lets the lifted thunder drop.

5 There for me the Saviour stands,
   Shows his wounds and spreads his hands,
   God is love! I know, I feel;
   Jesus weeps, and loves me still.

173. Lo! Round the Throne.

MARY L. DUNCAN. Tune, PARK STREET. L. M.

1. Lo! round the throne, a glorious band, The saints in countless myriads stand; Of ev'ry tongue redeemed to God, Arrayed in garments washed in blood, Arrayed in garments washed in blood.

2 Through tribulation great they came;
They bore the cross, despised the shame;
But now from all their labors rest,
In God's eternal glory blest.

3 They see the Saviour face to face;
They sing the triumph of his grace;
And day and night, with ceaseless praise,
To him their loud hosannas raise.

4 O may we tread the sacred road
That holy saints and martyrs trod;
Wage to the end the glorious strife,
And win, like them, a crown of life!

174. Now to the Lord.

1 Now to the Lord a noble song:
Awake, my soul, awake, my tongue;
Hosanna to the eternal name,
And all his boundless love proclaim.

2 See where it shines in Jesus' face,
The brightest image of his grace;
God, in the person of his Son,
Has all his mightiest works outdone.

3 The spacious earth and spreading flood
Proclaim the wise and powerful God;
And thy rich glories from afar
Sparkle in every rolling star.

4 Grace! 'tis a sweet, a charming theme,
My thoughts rejoice at Jesus name;
Ye angels, dwell upon the sound,
Ye heavens, reflect it to the ground.

5 Oh! may I reach that happy place,
Where he unveils his lovely face,
Where all his beauties you behold,
And sing his name to harps of gold.
—ISAAC WATTS.

175. Soon may the last glad song.

1 Soon may the last glad song arise,
Through all the millions of the skies;
That song of triumph which records
That all the earth is now the Lord's.

2 Let thrones, and powers, and kingdoms be
Obedient, mighty God, to thee;
And over land, and stream, and main,
Now wave the scepter of thy reign.

3 O let that glorious anthem swell;
Let host to host the triumph tell,
Till not one rebel heart remains,
But over all the Saviour reigns.
—Mrs. VOKE.

The Joyful Sound—L

176. Hail, Thou Once Despised.

JOHN BAKEWELL.   Tune, AUTUMN. 8, 7, d.

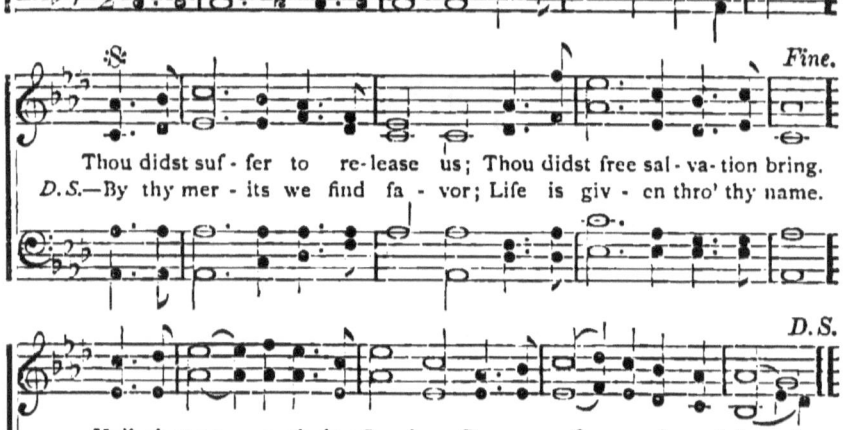

1. Hail, thou once de-spis-ed Jesus! Hail, thou Gal-i-le-an King!
Thou didst suf-fer to re-lease us; Thou didst free sal-va-tion bring.
D.S.—By thy mer-its we find fa-vor; Life is giv-en thro' thy name.
Hail, thou ag-o-niz-ing Sav-iour, Bearer of our sin and shame!

2 Paschal Lamb, by God appointed,
  All our sins on thee were laid:
By almighty love anointed,
  Thou hast full atonement made.
All thy people are forgiven,
  Through the virtue of thy blood;
Opened is the gate of heaven;
  Peace is made 'twixt man and God.

3 Jesus, hail! enthroned in glory,
  There forever to abide;
All the heavenly hosts adore thee,
  Seated at thy Father's side:
There for sinners thou art pleading;
  There thou dost our place prepare:
Ever for us interceding,
  Till in glory we appear.

4 Worship, honor, power, and blessing,
  Thou art worthy to receive:
Loudest praises, without ceasing,
  Meet it is for us to give.
Help, ye bright angelic spirits;
  Bring your sweetest, noblest lays;
Help to sing our Saviour's merits;
  Help to chant Immanuel's praise!

177. Love Divine.

1 Love divine, all love excelling,
  Joy of heaven, to earth come down!
Fix in us thy humble dwelling;
  All thy faithful mercies crown.
Jesus, thou art all compassion,
  Pure unbounded love thou art;
Visit us with thy salvation;
  Enter every trembling heart.

2 Come, almighty to deliver,
  Let us all thy life receive;
Suddenly return, and never,
  Never more thy temples leave:
Thee we would be always blessing,
  Serve thee as thy hosts above,
Pray, and praise thee without ceasing,
  Glory in thy perfect love.

3 Finish then thy new creation;
  Pure and spotless let us be;
Let us see thy great salvation,
  Perfectly restored in thee:
Changed from glory into glory,
  Till in heaven we take our place,
Till we cast our crowns before thee,
  Lost in wonder, love, and praise.

—C. WESLEY.

178. Jesus, I my Cross have Taken.

Henry F. Lyte.
Tune, ELLESDIE. 8, 7. d.

1. Jesus, I my cross have taken, All to leave and follow thee;
Naked, poor, despised, forsaken, Thou, from hence, my all shalt be:
Perish ev'ry fond ambition, All I've sought and hoped, and known;
Yet how rich is my condition, God and heaven are still my own!

2 Let the world despise and leave me,
They have left my Saviour, too;
Human hearts and looks deceive me;
Thou art not, like man, untrue;
And, while thou shalt smile upon me,
God of wisdom, love, and might,
Foes may hate, and friends may shun me;
Show thy face, and all is bright.

3 Go, then, earthly fame and treasure!
Come, disaster, scorn, and pain!
In thy service, pain is pleasure;
With thy favor, loss is gain.
I have called thee, "Abba, Father;"
I have stayed my heart on thee;
Storms may howl, and clouds may gather,
All must work for good to me.

4 Man may trouble and distress me,
'Twill but drive me to thy breast;
Life with trials hard may press me,
Heaven will bring me sweeter rest.
O 'tis not in grief to harm me,
While thy love is left to me;
O 'twere not in joy to charm me,
Were that joy unmixed with thee.

5 Know, my soul, thy full salvation;
Rise o'er sin, and fear, and care;
Joy to find in every station
Something still to do or bear.

Think what Spirit dwells within thee;
What a Father's smile is thine;
What a Saviour died to win thee:
Child of heaven, shouldst thou repine?

6 Haste thee on from grace to glory,
Armed by faith, and winged by prayer;
Heaven's eternal day's before thee,
God's own hand shall guide thee there.
Soon shall close thy earthly mission,
Swift shall pass thy pilgrim days,
Hope shall change to glad fruition,
Faith to sight, and prayer to praise.

179. Gently Lead Us.

1 Gently, Lord, oh, gently lead us
Through this lonely vale of tears,
Through the changes thou'st decreed us,
Till our last great change appears;
When temptation's darts assail us,
When in devious paths we stray,
Let thy goodness never fail us,
Lead us in thy perfect way.

2 In the hour of pain and anguish,
In the hour when death draws near,
Suffer not our hearts to languish,
Suffer not our souls to fear;
And when mortal life is ended,
Bid us in thine arms to rest,
Till by angel bands attended
We awake among the blest.

—Thos. Hastings.

180. I'll be There.

ISAAC WATTS. — Adapted by WM. J. KIRKPATRICK.

1. There is a land of pure delight, Where saints immortal reign:
   Infinite day excludes the night, And pleasures banish pain.
2. There everlasting spring abides, And never-with'ring flowers;
   Death, like a narrow sea, divides This heavenly land from ours.

REFRAIN.
I'll be there, I'll be there, When the first trumpet sounds I'll be there,
I'll be there, I'll be there, I'll be there, When the first trumpet sounds I'll be there.

3 Sweet fields beyond the swelling flood
Stand dressed in living green;
So to the Jews old Canaan stood,
While Jordan rolled between.

4 Could we but climb where Moses stood,
And view the landscape o'er, [flood
Not Jordan's stream, nor death's cold
Should fright us from the shore.

Copyright, 1887, by WM. J. KIRKPATRICK.

---

181. Down at the cross, where my Saviour died.

Key Ab.

1 Down at the cross, where my Saviour died,
Down where for cleansing from sin I cried;
There to my heart was the blood applied;
Glory to his name.

CHO.—Glory to his name,
Glory to his name,
There to my heart was the blood applied;
Glory to his name.

2 I am so wondrously saved from sin,
Jesus so sweetly abides within;
There at the cross where he took me in;
Glory to his name.

3 Oh, precious fountain, that saves from sin,
I am so glad I have entered in;
There Jesus saves me and keeps me clean,
Glory to his name.

4 Come to this fountain, so rich and sweet;
Cast thy poor soul at the Saviour's feet;
Plunge in to-day, and be made complete;
Glory to his name.

Forest. L. M.

182   O that my load of sin were gone.   L.M.

1 O that my load of sin were gone!
O that I could at last submit
At Jesus' feet to lay it down—
To lay my soul at Jesus' feet!

2 Rest for my soul I long to find:
Saviour of all, if mine thou art,
Give me thy meek and lowly mind,
And stamp thine image on my heart.

3 Break off the yoke of inbred sin,
And fully set my spirit free;

I cannot rest till pure within,
Till I am wholly lost in thee.

4 Fain would I learn of thee, my God,
Thy light and easy burden prove,
The cross all stained with hallowed blood,
The labor of thy dying love.

5 I would, but thou must give the power;
My heart from every sin release;
Bring near, bring near the joyful hour,
And fill me with thy perfect peace.
—CHAS. WESLEY.

183   Lord, I am Thine.   L.M.

1 Lord, I am thine, entirely thine,
Purchased and saved by blood divine;
With full consent thine would I be,
And own thy sovereign right in me.

2 Thine would I live, thine would I die;
Be thine through all eternity;
The vow is past, beyond repeal,
And now I set the solemn seal.

3 Here, at that cross where flows the blood
That bought my guilty soul for God,
Thee, my new Master now I call,
And consecrate to thee my all.

4 Do thou assist a feeble worm
The great engagement to perform;
Thy grace can full assistance lend,
And on that grace I dare depend.
—SAMUEL DAVIES.

184   I thirst, Thou wounded Lamb of God.   L. M.

1 I thirst, thou wounded Lamb of God,
To wash me in thy cleansing blood;
To dwell within thy wounds; then pain
Is sweet, and life or death is gain.

2 Take my poor heart, and let it be
Forever closed to all but thee:
Seal thou my breast, and let me wear
That pledge of love forever there.

3 How blest are they who still abide
Close sheltered in thy bleeding side!
Who thence their life and strength derive,
And by thee move, and in thee live.

4 What are our works but sin and death,
Till thou thy quickening Spirit breathe?
Thou giv'st the power thy grace to move;
O wondrous grace! O wondrous love!

5 How can it be, thou heavenly King,
That thou shouldst us to glory bring?
Make slaves the partners of thy throne,
Decked with a never-fading crown?

6 Hence our hearts melt, our eyes o'erflow,
Our words are lost, nor will we know,
Nor will we think of aught beside,
"My Lord, my Love is crucified."
—NICOLAUS L. ZINZENDORF.

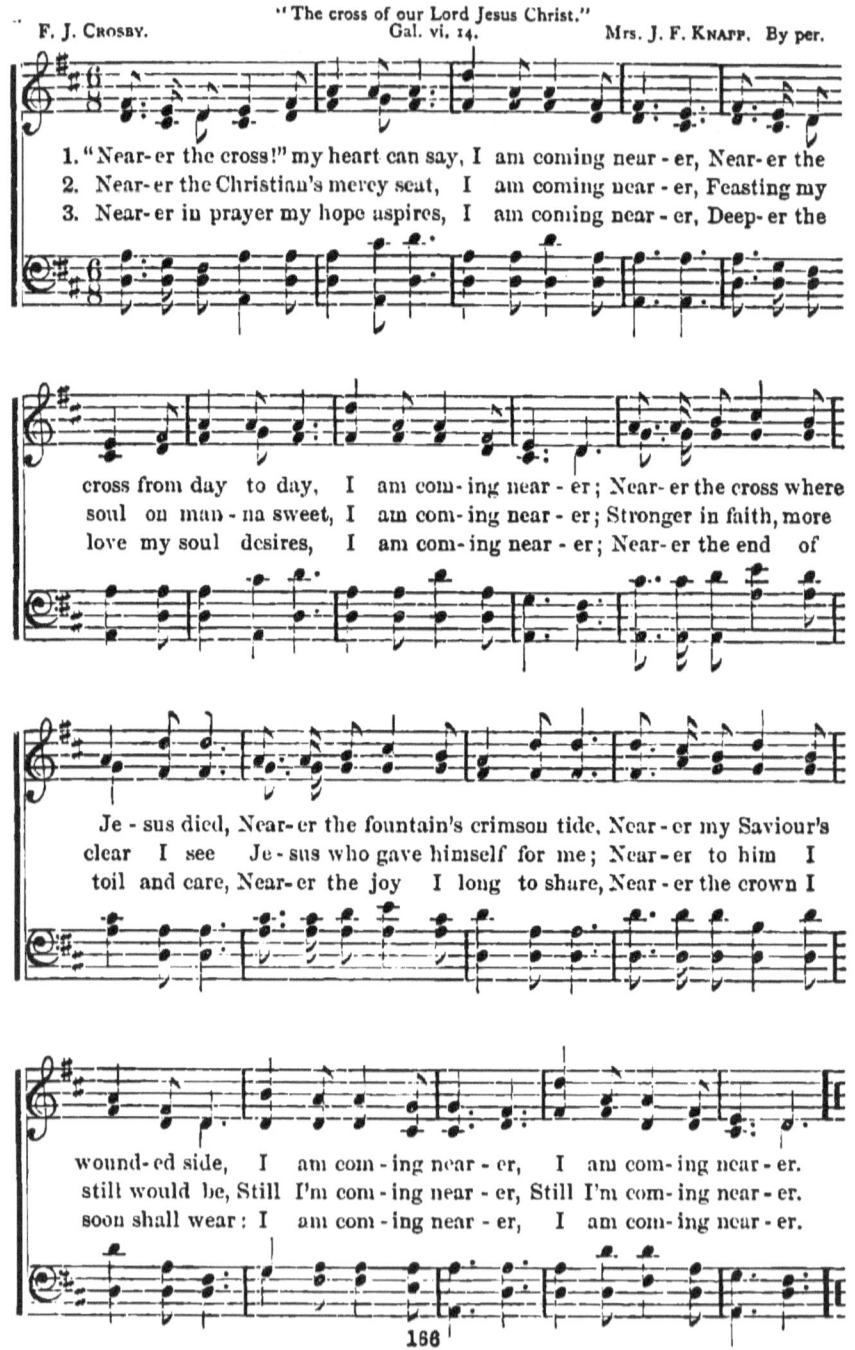

186. Till He Come.

"For yet a little while and he that shall come will come, and will not tarry."—Heb. x. 37.

Rev. Ed. H. Bickersteth.   Dr. Lowell Mason.

1. "Till he come!" Oh, let the words Linger on the trembling chords;
D.C.—Let us think how heaven and home Lie beyond that "Till he come!"

2. When the weary ones we love Enter on that rest above,
D.C.—Hush! be ev'ry murmur dumb, It is only "Till he come!"

Let the "little while" between In their golden light be seen;
When the words of love and cheer Fall no longer on our ear,

3 Clouds and darkness round us press;
Would we have one sorrow less?
All the sharpness of the cross,
All that tells the world is loss,
Death, and darkness, and the tomb,
Pain us only "Till he come!"

4 See, the feast of love is spread,
Drink the wine and eat the bread;
Sweet memorials, till the Lord
Call us round his heavenly board,
Some from earth, from glory some,
Severed only "Till he come!"

187. To-day the Saviour Calls.

Samuel Francis Smith.   Dr. Lowell Mason.

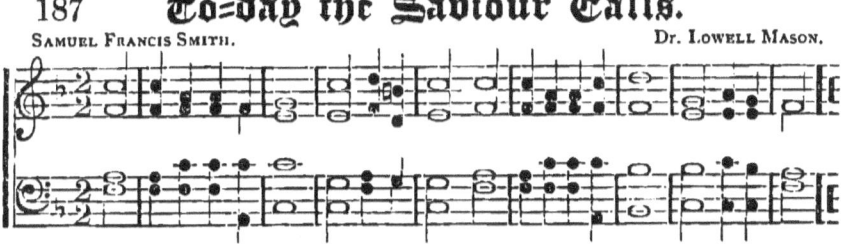

1 To-day the Saviour calls;
  Ye wand'rers, come;
  O ye benighted souls,
  Why longer roam?

2 To-day the Saviour calls;
  Oh, hear him now;
  Within these sacred walls
  To Jesus bow.

3 To-day the Saviour calls;
  For refuge fly;
  The storm of justice falls,
  And death is nigh.

4 The Spirit calls to-day;
  Yield to his power,
  Oh, grieve him not away,
  'Tis mercy's hour.

188. Come to Jesus.

1. Come to Jesus, Come to Jesus, Come to Jesus just now, Just now come to Jesus, Come to Jesus just now.

2 He will save you, etc.
3 He is able, etc.
4 He is willing, etc.
5 He is waiting, etc.
6 O believe him, etc.
7 He will bless you, etc.

189. Abide with Me.

HENRY F. LYTE.   Tune, EVENTIDE. 10s.

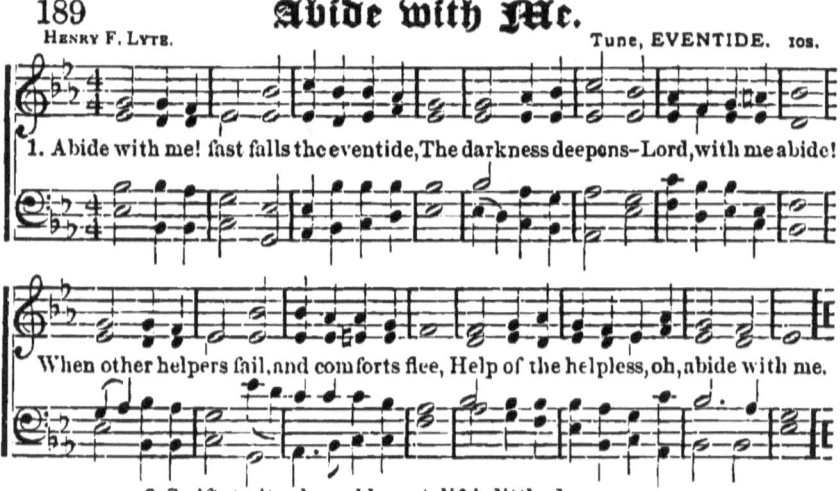

1. Abide with me! fast falls the eventide, The darkness deepens—Lord, with me abide! When other helpers fail, and comforts flee, Help of the helpless, oh, abide with me.

2 Swift to its close ebbs out life's little day;
Earth's joys grow dim, its glories pass away;
Change and decay in all around I see;
O thou, who changest not, abide with me!

3 I need thy presence every passing hour;
What but thy grace can foil the tempter's power?
Who, like thyself, my guide and stay can be?
Through cloud and sunshine, Lord, abide with me!

4 I fear no foe, with thee at hand to bless;
Ills have no weight, and tears no bitterness;
Where is death's sting? where, grave, thy victory?
I triumph still, if thou abide with me.

5 Hold thou thy cross before my closing eyes;
Shine through the gloom and point me to the skies;
Heaven's morning breaks, and earth's vain shadows flee;
In life, in death, O Lord, abide with me!

190. Come, Holy Spirit. ST. MARTIN'S. C. M.
I. Watts. Tune.

1. Come, Ho-ly Spir-it, heavenly Dove, With all thy quick'ning powers;
Kin-dle a flame of sa-cred love In these cold hearts of ours.

2 Look how we grovel here below,
   Fond of these earthly toys;
Our souls, how heavily they go,
   To reach eternal joys.

3 In vain we tune our formal songs,
   In vain we strive to rise;
Hosannas languish on our tongues,
   And our devotion dies.

4 Father, and shall we ever live
   At this poor dying rate,
Our love so faint, so cold to thee,
   And thine to us so great?

5 Come, Holy Spirit, heavenly Dove,
   With all thy quick'ning powers;
Come, shed abroad a Saviour's love,
   And that shall kindle ours.

191. Come, Ye Sinners. GREENVILLE. 8,7,4.
Joseph Hart. Tune.

Fine. *D.C.*

1 Come, ye sinners, poor and needy,
   Weak and wounded, sick and sore;
Jesus ready stands to save you,
   Full of pity, love, and power:
      He is able,
   He is willing: doubt no more.

2 Now, ye needy, come and welcome;
   God's free bounty glorify;
True belief and true repentance,
   Every grace that brings you nigh,
      Without money,
   Come to Jesus Christ and buy.

3 Let not conscience make you linger,
   Nor of fitness fondly dream;
All the fitness he requireth
   Is to feel your need of him
      This he gives you;
   'Tis the Spirit's glimmering beam.

4 Come, ye weary, heavy-laden,
   Bruised and mangled by the fall;
If you tarry till you're better,
   You will never come at all;
      Not the righteous—
   Sinners Jesus came to call.

5 Agonizing in the garden,
   Your Redeemer prostrate lies;
On the bloody tree behold him!
   Hear him cry, before he dies,
      "It is finished!"
   Sinners, will not this suffice?

6 Lo! the incarnate God, ascending,
   Pleads the merit of his blood;
Venture on him, venture freely;
   Let no other trust intrude:
      None but Jesus
   Can do helpless sinners good.

Ariel. C. P. M. Arr. by Lowell Mason.

192 O Love Divine.

1 O LOVE divine, how sweet thou art!
 When shall I find my willing heart
  All taken up by thee?
 I thirst, I faint, I die to prove
 The greatness of redeeming love,
  The love of Christ to me.

2 Stronger his love than death or hell;
 Its riches are unsearchable;
  The first-born sons of light
 Desire in vain its depths to see;
 They cannot reach the mystery,
  The length, the breadth, the height.

3 God only knows the love of God;
 O that it now were shed abroad
  In this poor stony heart!
 For love I sigh, for love I pine;
 This only portion, Lord, be mine;
  Be mine this better part.

4 O that I could forever sit
 With Mary at the Master's feet!
  Be this my happy choice;
 My only care, delight, and bliss,
 My joy, my heaven on earth, be this,
  To hear the Bridegroom's voice.

5 O that I could, with favored John,
 Recline my weary head upon
  The dear Redeemer's breast!
 From care, and sin, and sorrow free,
 Give me, O Lord, to find in thee
  My everlasting rest.

193 O could I Speak.

1 O COULD I speak the matchless worth,
 O could I sound the glories forth,
  Which in my Saviour shine,
 I'd soar and touch the heavenly strings,
 And vie with Gabriel while he sings
  In notes almost divine.

2 I'd sing the precious blood he spilt,
 My ransom from the dreadful guilt
  Of sin, and wrath divine;
 I'd sing his glorious righteousness,
 In which all-perfect, heavenly dress
  My soul shall ever shine.

3 I'd sing the characters he bears,
 And all the forms of love he wears,
  Exalted on his throne;
 In loftiest songs of sweetest praise,
 I would to everlasting days
  Make all his glories known.

4 Well, the delightful day will come
 When my dear Lord will bring me home,
  And I shall see his face;
 Then with my Saviour, Brother, Friend
 A blest eternity I'll spend,
  Triumphant in his grace.

Luther. S. M.   Dr. T. Hastings.

194   I love Thy kingdom.

1 I LOVE thy kingdom, Lord,
   The house of thine abode,
The Church our blest Redeemer saved
   With his own precious blood.

2 I love thy Church, O God!
   Her walls before thee stand,
Dear as the apple of thine eye,
   And graven on thy hand.

3 For her my tears shall fall,
   For her my prayers ascend:
To her my cares and toils be given,
   Till toils and cares shall end.

4 Beyond my highest joy
   I prize her heavenly ways,
Her sweet communion, solemn vows,
   Her hymns of love and praise.

5 Sure as thy truth shall last,
   To Zion shall be given
The brightest glories earth can yield,
   And brighter bliss of heaven.

195   Grace!

1 GRACE! 'tis a charming sound,
   Harmonious to the ear;
Heaven with the echo shall resound,
   And all the earth shall hear.

2 Grace first contrived a way
   To save rebellious man;
And all the steps that grace display,
   Which drew the wondrous plan.

3 Grace taught my roving feet
   To tread the heavenly road;
And new supplies each hour I meet,
   While pressing on to God.

4 Grace all the work shall crown
   Through everlasting days;
It lays in heaven the topmost stone,
   And well deserves our praise.

196   Stand up, and bless.

1 STAND up, and bless the Lord,
   Ye people of his choice;
Stand up, and bless the Lord your God,
   With heart, and soul, and voice.

2 Though high above all praise,
   Above all blessing high,
Who would not fear his holy name,
   And laud, and magnify?

3 O for the living flame
   From his own altar brought,
To touch our lips, our souls inspire,
   And wing to heaven our thought!

4 God is our strength and song,
   And his salvation ours;
Then be his love in Christ proclaimed
   With all our ransomed powers.

5 Stand up, and bless the Lord;
   The Lord your God adore;
Stand up, and bless his glorious name,
   Henceforth, forevermore.

197   Purity of heart.

1 BLEST are the pure in heart,
   For they shall see our God;
The secret of the Lord is theirs;
   Their soul is his abode.

2 Still to the lowly soul
   He doth himself impart,
And for his temple and his throne
   Selects the pure in heart.

3 Lord, we thy presence seek,
   May ours this blessing be;
O give the pure and lowly heart,—
   A temple meet for thee.

Doxology. S. M.

To God, the Father, Son,
   And Spirit, One in Three,
Be glory, as it was, is now,
   And shall forever be.

198. Come, Ye Disconsolate.

THOMAS MOORE, alt., and THOS. HASTINGS. SAMUEL WEBBE.

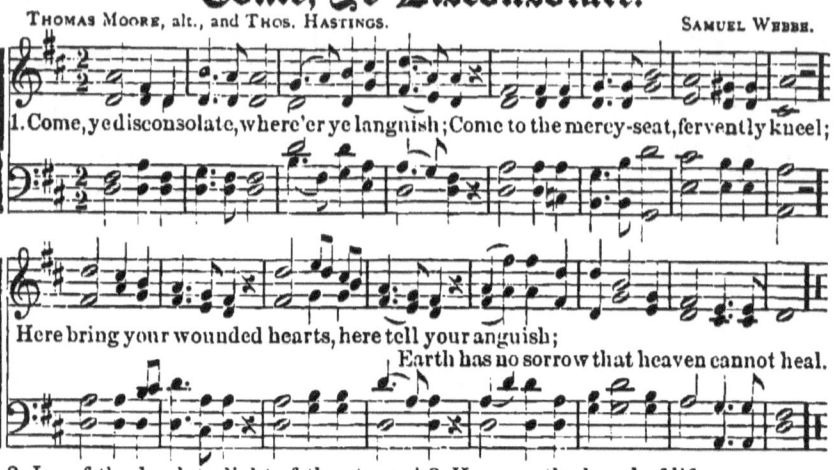

1. Come, ye disconsolate, where'er ye languish; Come to the mercy-seat, fervently kneel;
Here bring your wounded hearts, here tell your anguish;
Earth has no sorrow that heaven cannot heal.

2 Joy of the desolate, light of the straying,
Hope of the penitent, fadeless and pure,
Here speaks the Comforter, tenderly saying,
"Earth has no sorrow that heaven cannot cure."

3 Here see the bread of life; see waters flowing
Forth from the throne of God, pure from above; [knowing
Come to the feast of love; come, ever
Earth has no sorrow but heaven can [remove.

199. At the Fountain.

OLD MELODY.

CHORUS.

1 Of him who did salvation bring,
I'm at the fountain drinking,
I could forever think and sing,
I'm on my journey home.
CHO—Glory to God,
I'm at the fountain drinking,
Glory to God,
I'm on my journey home.

2 Ask but his grace and lo! 'tis given,
I'm at the fountain drinking,
Ask and he turns your hell to heaven,
I'm on my journey home.

3 Tho' sin and sorrow wound my soul,
I'm at the fountain drinking,
Jesus, thy balm will make me whole,
I'm on my journey home.

4 Where'er I am, where'er I move,
I'm at the fountain drinking,
I meet the object of my love,
I'm on my journey home.

5 Insatiate to this spring I fly,
I'm at the fountain drinking,
I drink and yet am ever dry,
I'm on my journey home.
CHO.—Glory to God,
I'm at the fountain drinking,
Glory to God,
My soul is satisfied.

Alida. C. M. Double. D. B. Thompson.

200. How happy every child.

1 How happy every child of grace,
 Who knows his sins forgiven!
"This earth," he cries, "is not my place,
 I seek my place in heaven,—
A country far from mortal sight;
 Yet O, by faith I see
The land of rest, the saints' delight,
 The heaven prepared for me."

2 O what a blessed hope is ours!
 While here on earth we stay,
We more than taste the heavenly
 And antedate that day; [powers,
We feel the resurrection near,
 Our life in Christ concealed,
And with his glorious presence here
 Our earthen vessels filled.

3 O would he more of heaven bestow,
 And let the vessels break,
And let our ransomed spirits go
 To grasp the God we seek;
In rapturous awe on him to gaze,
 Who bought the sight for me;
And shout and wonder at his grace
 Through all eternity!

201. I heard the voice of Jesus.

1 I HEARD the voice of Jesus say,
 "Come unto me and rest;
Lay down, thou weary one, lay down
 Thy head upon my breast!"
I came to Jesus as I was,
 Weary, and worn, and sad,
I found in him a resting-place,
 And he hath made me glad.

2 I heard the voice of Jesus say,
 "Behold, I freely give
The living water; thirsty one,
 Stoop down, and drink, and live!"
I came to Jesus, and I drank
 Of that life-giving stream;
My thirst was quenched, my soul re-
 And now I live in him. [vived,

3 I heard the voice of Jesus say,
 "I am this dark world's light;
Look unto me, thy morn shall rise
 And all thy day be bright!"
I looked to Jesus, and I found
 In him my Star, my Sun;
And in that light of life I'll walk,
 Till all my journey's done.

202. Work, for the night is coming.

1 WORK, for the night is coming,
 Work through the morning hours;
Work, while the dew is sparkling,
 Work 'mid springing flowers;
Work, when the day grows brighter,
 Work in the glowing sun;
Work, for the night is coming,
 When man's work is done.

2 Work, for the night is coming,
 Work through the sunny noon;
Fill brightest hours with labor,
 Rest comes sure and soon,
Give every flying minute
 Something to keep in store:
Work, for the night is coming,
 When man works no more.

3 Work, for the night is coming,
 Under the sunset skies;
While their bright tints are glowing,
 Work, for daylight flies.
Work till the last beam fadeth,
 Fadeth to shine no more;
Work while the night is darkening,
 When man's work is o'er.

203. Sweet Land of Rest.

1. Sweet land of rest, for thee I sigh! When will the moment come,
D.C.—And dwell with Christ at home, . . . And dwell with Christ at home;
2. No tran-quil joys on earth I know, No peaceful, sheltering dome;
D.C.—This world is not my home, . . . This world is not my home;

When I shall lay my ar-mor by, And dwell with Christ at home.
This world's a wil-der-ness of woe, This world is not my home.

3 To Jesus Christ I sought for rest,
  He bade me cease to roam;
  But fly for succor to his breast,
  And he'd conduct me home.

4 Weary of wand'ring round and round
  This vale of sin and gloom,
  I long to leave th'unhallowed ground,
  And dwell with Christ at home.

204. Only Trust Him.

J. H. S.
"Take my yoke upon you, and learn of me; and ye shall find rest unto your souls."—Matt. xi. 29.
Rev. J. H. STOCKTON. By per.

1. Come, ev'ry soul by sin oppressed, There's mercy with the Lord, And he will surely
2. For Jesus shed his precious blood Rich blessings to bestow; Plunge now into the
3. Yes, Jesus is the Truth, the Way, That leads you into rest; Believe in him with-
4. Come then, and join this holy band, And on to glory go, To dwell in that ce-

CHORUS.

give you rest, By trusting in his word. On-ly trust him, only trust him,
crimson flood That washes white as snow. *Second Chorus—*
out de-lay, And you are ful-ly blest. Come to Je-sus, come to Je-sus,
lestial land, Where joys immortal flow.

Only Trust Him.—CONCLUDED.

Only trust him now; He will save you, he will save you, He will save you now.
Come to Jesus now;

205. Jesus is Mine!

"My beloved is mine."—S of Sol. ii. 16.

Mrs. CATHARINE J. BONAR.   T. E. PERKINS. By per.

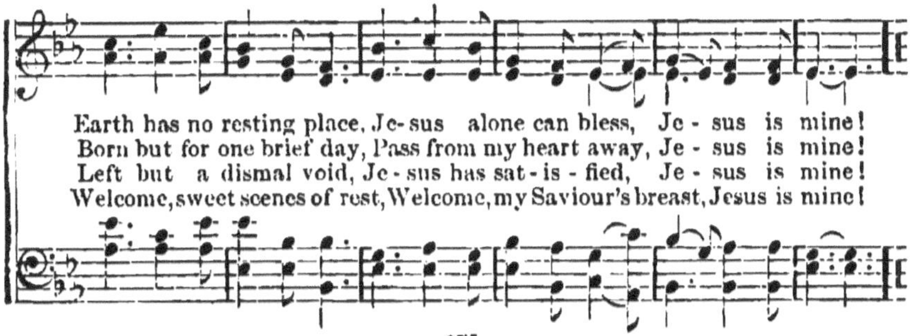

1. Fade, fade, each earth-ly joy, Je-sus is mine! Break, ev-'ry tender tie, Je-sus is mine! Dark is the wilderness, Earth has no resting place, Je-sus alone can bless, Je-sus is mine!
2. Tempt not my soul a-way, Je-sus is mine! Here would I ev-er stay, Je-sus is mine! Per-ish-ing things of clay, Born but for one brief day, Pass from my heart away, Je-sus is mine!
3. Fare-well, ye dreams of night, Je-sus is mine! Lost in this dawning light, Je-sus is mine! All that my soul has tried Left but a dismal void, Je-sus has sat-is-fied, Je-sus is mine!
4. Fare-well, mor-tal-i-ty, Je-sus is mine! Welcome, e-ter-ni-ty, Je-sus is mine! Welcome, O loved and blest, Welcome, sweet scenes of rest, Welcome, my Saviour's breast, Jesus is mine!

Zerah. C. M.

Dr. L. Mason.

206 *Come, ye that love.*

1 COME, ye that love the Saviour's name,
  And joy to make it known,
The Sovereign of your hearts proclaim,
  And bow before his throne.

2 Behold your Lord, your Master crowned
  With glories all divine;
And tell the wondering nations round
  How bright those glories shine.

3 When, in his earthly courts, we view
  The glories of our King,
We long to love as angels do,
  And wish like them to sing.

4 And shall we long and wish in vain?
  Lord, teach our songs to rise:
Thy love can animate the strain,
  And bid it reach the skies.

207 *What glory gilds.*

1 WHAT glory gilds the sacred page!
  Majestic, like the sun,
It gives a light to every age;
  It gives, but borrows none.

2 The power that gave it still supplies
  The gracious light and heat;
Its truths upon the nations rise;
  They rise, but never set.

3 Lord, everlasting thanks be thine
  For such a bright display,
As makes a world of darkness shine
  With beams of heavenly day.

4 My soul rejoices to pursue
  The steps of him I love,
Till glory breaks upon my view
  In brighter worlds above.

208 *The Prince of Peace.*

1 To us a Child of hope is born,
  To us a Son is given;
Him shall the tribes of earth obey,
  Him, all the hosts of heaven.

2 His name shall be the Prince of Peace,
  Forevermore adored;
The Wonderful, the Counselor,
  The great and mighty Lord.

3 His power, increasing, still shall spread;
  His reign no end shall know;
Justice shall guard his throne above,
  And peace abound below.

4 To us a Child of hope is born,
  To us a Son is given;
The Wonderful, the Counselor,
  The mighty Lord of heaven.

209 *The joyful sound.*

1 SALVATION! O the joyful sound
  What pleasure to our ears!
A sovereign balm for every wound,
  A cordial for our fears.

2 Salvation! let the echo fly
  The spacious earth around,
While all the armies of the sky
  Conspire to raise the sound.

3 Salvation! O thou bleeding Lamb!
  To thee the praise belongs:
Salvation shall inspire our hearts,
  And dwell upon our tongues.

Doxology. C. M.

To Father, Son, and Holy Ghost,
  The God whom we adore,
Be glory, as it was, is now,
  And shall be evermore.

210. Beyond the Smiling.

H. Bonar. — W. A. Tarbutton.

1 Beyond the smiling and the weeping,
   I shall be soon;
  Beyond the waking and the sleeping,
  Beyond the sowing and the reaping,
   I shall be soon.

2 Beyond the blooming and the fading,
   I shall be soon;
  Beyond the shining and the shading,
  Beyond the hoping and the dreading,
   I shall be soon.

3 Beyond the rising and the setting,
   I shall be soon;
  Beyond the calming and the fretting,
  Beyond remembering and forgetting,
   I shall be soon.

4 Beyond the parting and the meeting,
   I shall be soon;
  Beyond the farewell and the greeting,
  Beyond the pulse's fever beating,
   I shall be soon.

211. Gloria Patri.

C. Norris.

The Joyful Sound—M

Antioch. C. M.

212 O for a thousand tongues.

1 O FOR a thousand tongues, to sing
My great Redeemer's praise;
The glories of my God and King,
The triumphs of his grace!

2 My gracious Master and my God,
Assist me to proclaim,
To spread through all the earth abroad,
The honors of thy name.

3 Jesus! the name that charms our fears,
That bids our sorrows cease;
'Tis music in the sinner's ears,
'Tis life, and health, and peace.

4 He breaks the power of canceled sin,
He sets the prisoner free;
His blood can make the foulest clean;
His blood availed for me.

5 He speaks, and, listening to his voice,
New life the dead receive;
The mournful, broken hearts rejoice;
The humble poor believe.

6 Hear him, ye deaf; his praise, ye dumb,
Your loosened tongues employ;
Ye blind, behold your Saviour come;
And leap, ye lame, for joy.

213 Joy to the world.

1 Joy to the world! the Lord is come;
Let earth receive her King;
Let every heart prepare him room,
And heaven and nature sing.

2 Joy to the world! the Saviour reigns;
Let men their songs employ;
While fields and floods, rocks, hills and plains,
Repeat the sounding joy.

3 No more let sin and sorrow grow,
Nor thorns infest the ground;
He comes to make his blessings flow
Far as the curse is found.

4 He rules the world with truth and grace,
And makes the nations prove
The glories of his righteousness,
And wonders of his love.

214 Evils of Intemperance. Tune, BOYLSTON.

1 MOURN for the thousands slain,
The youthful and the strong;
Mourn for the wine-cup's fearful reign,
And the deluded throng.

2 Mourn for the ruined soul—
Eternal life and light
Lost by the fiery, maddening bowl,
And turned to hopeless night.

3 Mourn for the lost,—but call,
Call to the strong, the free;
Rouse them to shun that dreadful fall,
And to the refuge flee.

4 Mourn for the lost,—but pray,
Pray to our God above,
To break the fell destroyer's sway,
And show his saving love.

215 What Ruin! Tune, EVAN.

1 WHAT ruin hath intemperance wrought!
How widely roll its waves!
How many myriads hath it brought
To fill dishonored graves!

2 And see, O Lord, what numbers still
Are maddened by the bowl,
Led captive at the tyrant's will
In bondage, heart and soul.

3 Stretch forth thy hand, O God, our King,
And break the galling chain;
Deliverance to the captive bring,
And end the usurper's reign.

4 The cause of temperance is thine own;
Our plans and efforts bless;
We trust, O Lord, in thee alone
To crown them with success.

216. Gathering Home.

Miss Mariana B. Slade. R. N. M'Intosh. By per.

1. Up to the bounti-ful Giv-er of life,—Gathering home! gathering home!
2. Up to the city where falleth no night,—Gathering home! gathering home!
3. Up to the beautiful mansions above,—Gathering home! gathering home!

Up to the dwelling where cometh no strife, The dear ones are gathering home.
Up where the Saviour's own face is the light, The dear ones are gathering home.
Safe in the arms of his in-finite love, The dear ones are gathering home.

CHORUS.

Gath-er-ing home! . . . . gath-er-ing home! . . . .
  Gath-er-ing home!   gath-er-ing home!
Nev-er to sorrow more, never to roam; Gathering home! . . . .
                                          Gath-er-ing home!
gath-er-ing home! . . . . God's children are gather-ing home.
  gath-er-ing home!

217. The Lord's Garden.

Tune, GARDEN.

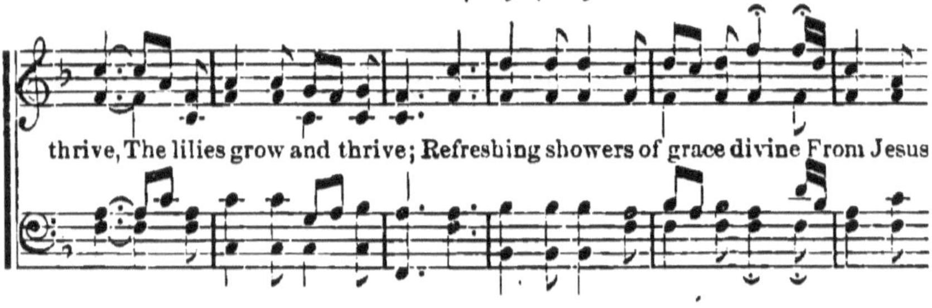

1. The Lord into his garden comes,
The spices yield their rich perfumes, The lilies grow and thrive, The lilies grow and thrive; Refreshing showers of grace divine From Jesus flow to ev-'ry vine, And make the dead revive, And make the dead revive.

2 O that this dry and barren ground
In springs of water may abound,—
A fruitful soil become;
The desert blossoms like the rose,
When Jesus conquers all his foes,
And makes his people one.

3 Come, brethren, you that love the Lord,
Who taste the sweetness of his word,
In Jesus' ways go on;
Our troubles and our trials here,
Will only make us richer there,
When we arrive at home.

218. Holy, holy, holy.

REGINALD HEBER.

Tune, NICEA. 11, 12, 10.

1. Ho-ly, ho-ly, ho-ly, Lord God Almight-y! Ear-ly in the
2. Ho-ly, ho-ly, ho-ly! all the saints adore thee, Casting down their
3. Ho-ly, ho-ly, ho-ly! tho' the darkness hide thee, Tho' the eye of
4. Ho-ly, ho-ly, ho-ly, Lord God Almight-y! All thy works shall

Holy, holy, holy.—CONCLUDED.

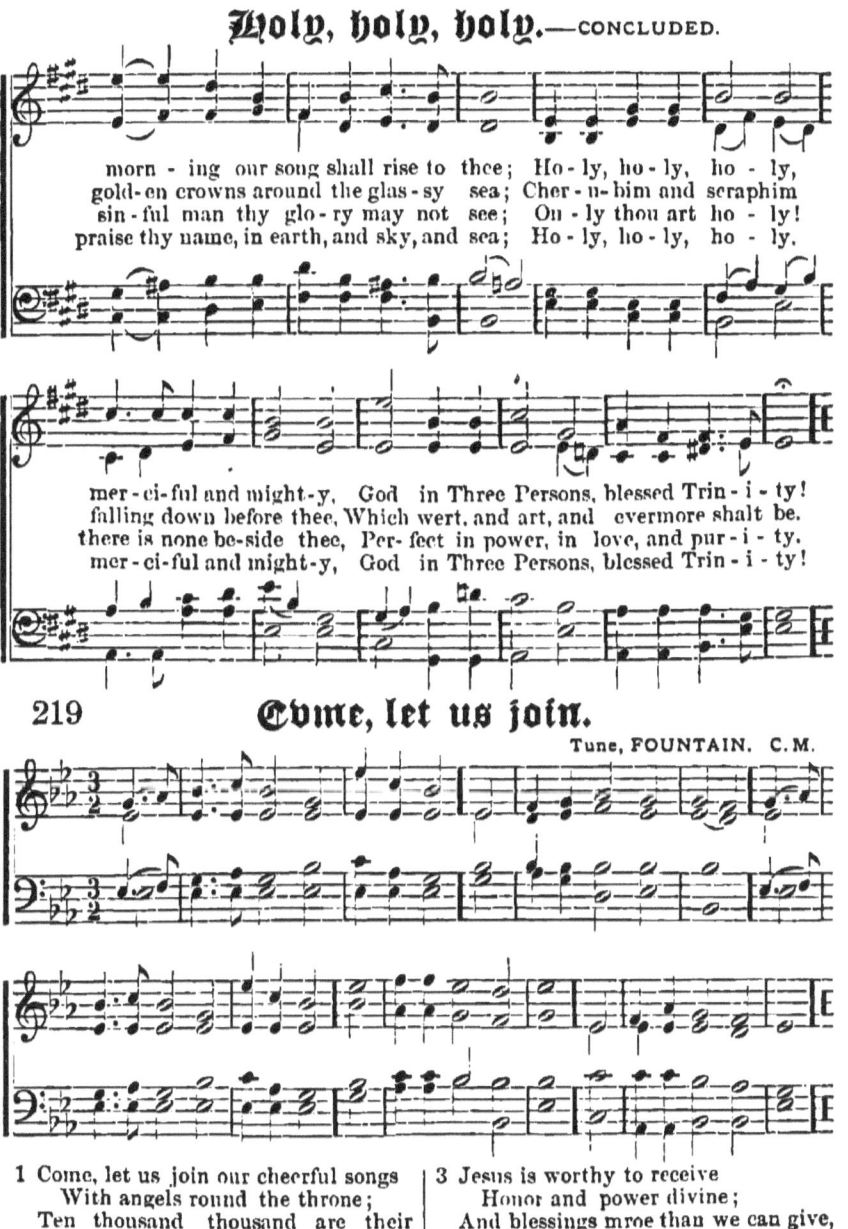

morn - ing our song shall rise to thee; Ho - ly, ho - ly, ho - ly,
gold- en crowns around the glas - sy sea; Cher - u- bim and seraphim
sin - ful man thy glo - ry may not see; On - ly thou art ho - ly!
praise thy name, in earth, and sky, and sea; Ho - ly, ho - ly, ho - ly.

mer - ci-ful and might-y, God in Three Persons, blessed Trin - i - ty!
falling down before thee, Which wert, and art, and evermore shalt be.
there is none be-side thee, Per- fect in power, in love, and pur - i - ty.
mer - ci-ful and might-y, God in Three Persons, blessed Trin - i - ty!

219 **Come, let us join.**

Tune, FOUNTAIN. C. M.

1 Come, let us join our cheerful songs
   With angels round the throne;
   Ten thousand thousand are their [tongues,
   But all their joys are one.

2 "Worthy the Lamb that died," they
   "To be exalted thus!" [cry,
   "Worthy the Lamb!" our hearts reply,
   "For he was slain for us."

3 Jesus is worthy to receive
   Honor and power divine;
   And blessings mroe than we can give,
   Be, Lord, forever thine.

4 The whole creation join in one,
   To bless the sacred name
   Of him that sits upon the throne,
   And to adore the Lamb.

220 The Morning Light.

SAMUEL F. SMITH. Tune, WEBB. 7, 6.

1 The morning light is breaking;
  The darkness disappears;
  The sons of earth are waking
  To penitential tears;
  Each breeze that sweeps the ocean
  Brings tidings from afar,
  Of nations in commotion,
  Prepared for Zion's war.

2 See heathen nations bending
  Before the God we love,
  And thousand hearts ascending
  In gratitude above;
  While sinners, now confessing,
  The gospel call obey,
  And seek the Saviour's blessing,
  A nation in a day.

3 Blest river of salvation,
  Pursue thine onward way;
  Flow thou to every nation,
  Nor in thy richness stay:
  Stay not till all the lowly
  Triumphant reach their home;
  Stay not till all the holy
  Proclaim, "The Lord is come!"

221 Stand up, stand up for Jesus.

GEO. DUFFIELD, Jr. Tune above.

1 STAND up, stand up for Jesus,
  Ye soldiers of the cross;
  Lift high his royal banner,
  It must not suffer loss;
  From victory unto victory
  His army shall he lead
  Till every foe is vanquished
  And Christ is Lord indeed.

2 Stand up, stand up for Jesus,
  The trumpet call obey;
  Forth to the mighty conflict,
  In this his glorious day:
  "Ye that are men, now serve him,"
  Against unnumbered foes:
  Your courage rise with danger,
  And strength to strength oppose.

3 Stand up, stand up for Jesus,
  Stand in his strength alone;
  The arm of flesh will fail you;
  Ye dare not trust your own:
  Put on the gospel armor,
  Each piece put on with prayer;
  Where duty calls, or danger,
  Be never wanting there.

4 Stand up, stand up for Jesus,
  The strife will not be long;
  This day the noise of battle,
  The next the victor's song:
  To him that overcometh,
  A crown of life shall be;
  He with the King of glory
  Shall reign eternally.

222 Awake, My Soul.

MEDLEY. Tune, LOVING-KINDNESS. L.M.

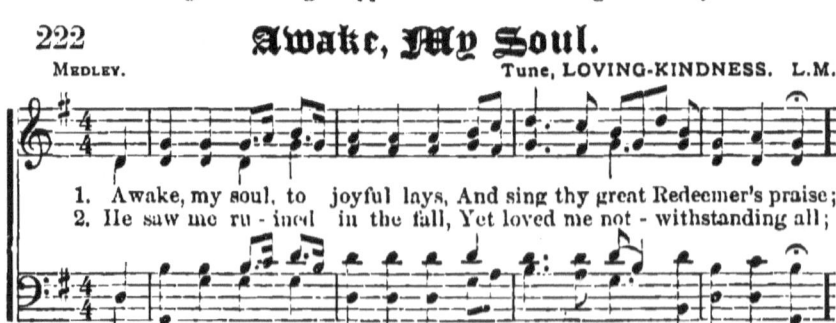

1. Awake, my soul, to joyful lays, And sing thy great Redeemer's praise;
2. He saw me ru-ined in the fall, Yet loved me not-withstanding all;

Awake, My Soul.—CONCLUDED.

He just-ly claims a song from me, His lov-ing-kind-ness, oh, how free!
He saved me from my lost e-state, His lov-ing-kind-ness, oh, how great!

Lov-ing-kindness, lov-ing-kindness, His lov-ing-kind-ness, oh, how free!
Lov-ing-kindness, lov-ing-kindness, His lov-ing-kind-ness, oh, how great!

3 Though num'rous hosts of mighty foes,
Though earth and hell my way oppose,
He safely leads my soul along,
His loving-kindness, oh, how strong!

4 When trouble, like a gloomy cloud,
Has gathered thick, and thundered loud,
He near my soul has always stood,
His loving-kindness, oh, how good!

223 My Faith Looks Up to Thee.

RAY PALMER.   L. MASON.

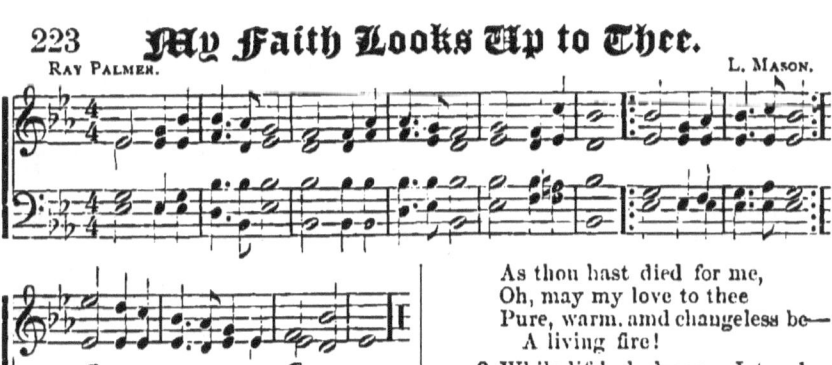

1 My faith looks up to thee,
Thou Lamb of Calvary,
  Saviour divine!
Now hear me while I pray;
Take all my guilt away;
Oh, let me from this day
  Be wholly thine!

2 May thy rich grace impart
Strength to my fainting heart,
  My zeal inspire!
As thou hast died for me,
Oh, may my love to thee
Pure, warm, and changeless be—
  A living fire!

3 While life's dark maze I tread,
And griefs around me spread,
  Be thou my guide;
Bid darkness turn to day,
Wipe sorrow's tears away,
Nor let me ever stray
  From thee aside.

4 When ends life's transient dream,
When death's cold sullen stream
  Shall o'er me roll,
Blest Saviour! then, in love,
Fear and distrust remove;
Oh, bear me safe above—
  A ransomed soul!

224. Happy Day.

P. DODDRIDGE. English Melody.

1. O happy day, that fixed my choice On thee, my Saviour and my God!
Well may this glowing heart rejoice, And tell its raptures all abroad.
Happy day, happy day, When Jesus washed my sins away!
He taught me how to watch and pray, And live rejoicing ev'ry day.

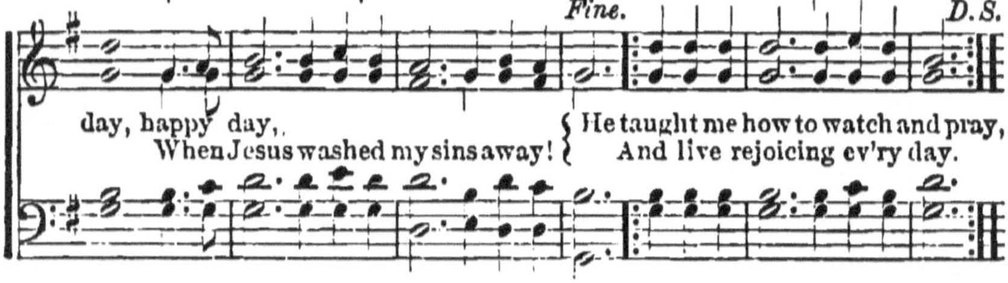

2 O happy bond, that seals my vows
To him who merits all my love!
Let cheerful anthems fill his house,
While to that sacred shrine I move.

3 'Tis done! the great transaction's done!
I am my Lord's, and he is mine:
He drew me, and I followed on,
Charmed to confess that voice divine.

4 Now rest, my long-divided heart;
Fixed on this blissful center, rest;
Nor ever from thy Lord depart;
With him of every good possessed.

5 High heav'n that heard the solemn vow,
That vow renewed shall daily hear,
Till in life's latest hour I bow,
And bless in death a bond so dear.

225. He Came to Save Me.

H. E. BLAIR. WM. J. KIRKPATRICK.

1. When Jesus laid his crown aside, He came to save me;
When on the cross he bled and died, ... He came to save me.
2. In my poor heart he deigns to dwell, He came to save me;
Oh, praise his name, I know it well, ... He came to save me.

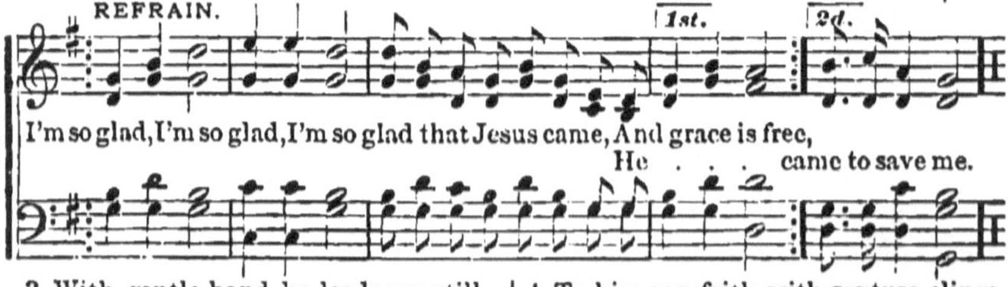

REFRAIN.
I'm so glad, I'm so glad, I'm so glad that Jesus came, And grace is free,
He . . . came to save me.

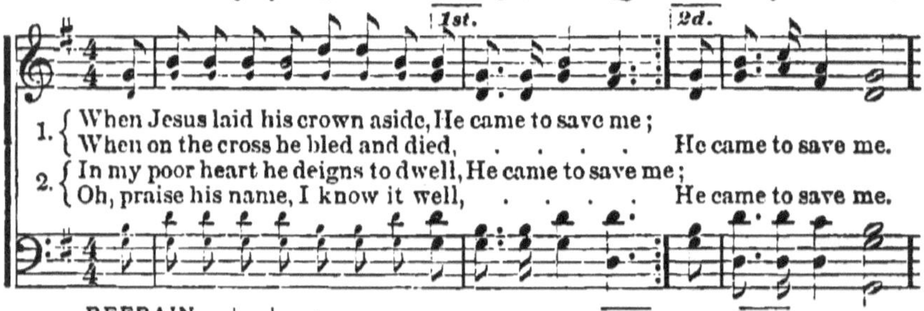

3 With gentle hand he leads me still,
He came to save me;
And trusting him I fear no ill,
He came to save me.

4 To him my faith with rapture clings,
He came to save me;
To him my heart looks up and sings,
He came to save me.

Copyright, 1866, by WM. J. KIRKPATRICK.

226. Revive us again.

WM. P. MACKAY.   J. J. HUSBAND.

1. We praise thee, O God! for the Son of thy love,
For Jesus who died and is now gone above.

REFRAIN.
Hal-le-lujah! thine the glory; Halle-lujah! a-men! Revive us a-gain.

2 We praise thee, O God! for thy Spirit of light,
Who has shown us our Saviour and scattered our night.
3 All glory and praise to the Lamb that was slain,
Who has borne all our sins, and has cleansed every stain.
4 All glory and praise to the God of all grace,
Who has bought us, and sought us, and guided our ways.
5 Revive us again; fill each heart with thy love;
May each soul be rekindled with fire from above.

227. All for Jesus.

MARY D JAMES.   Arranged.

1. { All for Jesus! all for Je-sus! All my being's ransomed powers:
    All my thoughts, and words, and doings, All my days, and all my hours.
2. { Let my hands perform his bidding, Let my feet run in his ways—
    Let my eyes see Jesus on - ly, Let my lips speak forth his praise,

All for Jesus! all for Je - sus! All my days, and all my hours; hours.
All for Jesus! all for Je - sus! Let my lips speak forth his praise; praise.

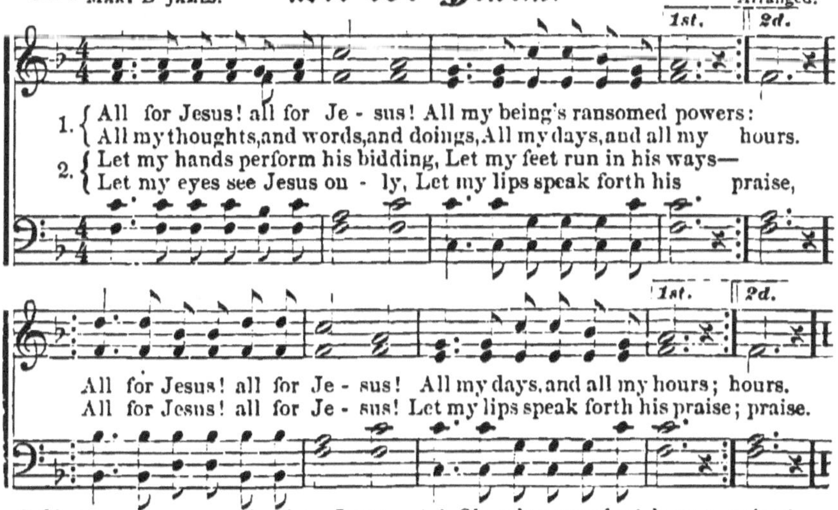

3 Since my eyes were fixed on Jesus,
I've lost sight of all besides;
So enchained my spirit's vision,
Looking at the Crucified.
|: All for Jesus! all for Jesus!
Looking at the Crucified. :||

4 Oh, what wonder! how amazing!
Jesus, glorious King of kings—
Deigns to call me his beloved,
Lets me rest beneath his wings.
|: All for Jesus! all for Jesus!
Resting now beneath his wings! :||

185

228. Shall We Pray for You?

E. E. Hewitt — Jno. R. Sweney.

1. When we come with burdened souls And before our Father bow,
Shall we pray for you, dear friend? Shall we plead for you just now?
2. Shall we ask a living faith, And a new and better heart?
That the Holy Spirit now May renewing grace impart?

CHORUS.

Shall we pray for you? While our heart-petitions blend, for you?
Coming in the Saviour's name, Shall we pray for you, dear friend?

3 Are you willing we should know
That you long for peace within?
Do you seek the Lord indeed,
And the power that saves from sin?

4 Come and join us in our prayer;
Low before the Saviour bow;
While he waits to hear your voice,
Give yourself to Jesus now.

Copyright, 1889, by Jno. R. Sweney.

229. Nearer to Thee.

Martha J. Lankton — Wm. J. Kirkpatrick.

1. When doubt and conflict weigh me down, and | clouds before me | rise,
Whose gath'ring gloom and deep'ning shade With | sorrow fills mine | eyes,
2. When joys that once I thought so true Have | lost each balmy | sweet,
And withered hopes, like summer flowers, Lie | crushed beneath my | feet,
3. While day by day I journey on To . . . . | reach that world sub- | lime,
That stands in perfect loveliness Be - - - | yond the shore of | time;

Copyright, 1887, by John J. Hood.

Nearer to Thee.—CONCLUDED.

'Tis then I lift my fainting soul In . . . prayer that I may be
With quivering lip and yearning heart I pray on bend-ed knee,
My faith looks up and softly breathes The prayer so dear to me,

Lento.

Near - - er, my God, to thee, Near - - er to thee.

230 Better Farther On.

Arr. by JAMES NICHOLSON. L. THOMPSON.

1. Oft I hear hope sweetly singing, Soft-ly in an un-der-tone;

Fine.

Sing-ing as if God had taught her—It is bet-ter far-ther on.
D.S.—Sings it so my heart may hear it— It is bet-ter far-ther on.

D.S.

Night and day she sings this same song—Sings it while I sit a-lone,

2 When my faith took hold on Jesus,
　Light divine within me shone,
　And I know since that glad moment,
　　"It is better farther on."
　Daily coming to the fountain,
　Flowing free for every one,
　I am saved, and hope is singing—
　　"It is better farther on."

3 Farther on! but how much farther?
　Count the milestones one by one;
　No, no counting, only trusting—
　　"It is better farther on."
　Hope, my soul, hope on forever,
　All thy doubts and fears be gone,
　Jesus will forsake thee never—
　　"It is better farther on."

Copyright, 1875, in "Precious Songs."

Pleyel's Hymn. 7s. — IGNACE PLEYEL.

231 Gracious Spirit, love divine.

1 GRACIOUS Spirit, love divine,
  Let thy light within me shine!
  All my guilty fears remove;
  Fill me with thy heavenly love.

2 Speak thy pardoning grace to me;
  Set the burdened sinner free;
  Lead me to the Lamb of God;
  Wash me in his precious blood.

3 Life and peace to me impart;
  Seal salvation on my heart;
  Breathe thyself into my breast,
  Earnest of immortal rest.

4 Let me never from thee stray;
  Keep me in the narrow way;
  Fill my soul with joy divine;
  Keep me, Lord, forever thine.

232 Holy Ghost, with light divine.

1 HOLY GHOST, with light divine,
  Shine upon this heart of mine;
  Chase the shades of night away,
  Turn my darkness into day.

2 Holy Ghost, with power divine,
  Cleanse this guilty heart of mine;
  Long hath sin, without control,
  Held dominion o'er my soul.

3 Holy Ghost, with joy divine,
  Cheer this saddened heart of mine;
  Bid my many woes depart,
  Heal my wounded, bleeding heart.

4 Holy Spirit, all divine,
  Dwell within this heart of mine;
  Cast down every idol-throne,
  Reign supreme—and reign alone.

Rockingham. L. M. — LOWELL MASON.

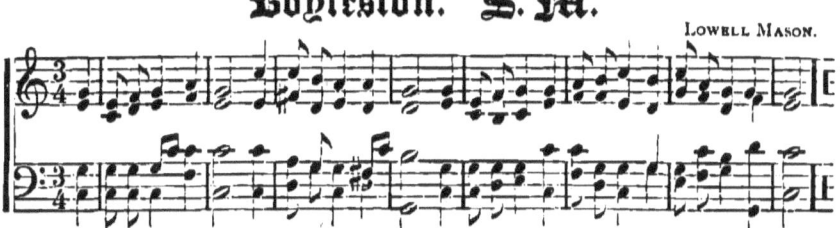

Boylston. S. M.
LOWELL MASON.

233 Lord, God, the Holy Ghost.

1 LORD, God, the Holy Ghost!
In this accepted hour,
As on the day of Pentecost,
Descend in all thy power.

2 We meet with one accord
In our appointed place,
And wait the promise of our Lord,—
The Spirit of all grace.

3 Like mighty, rushing wind
Upon the waves beneath,
Move with one impulse every mind;
One soul, one feeling breathe.

4 The young, the old, inspire
With wisdom from above;   [fire,
And give us hearts and tongues of
To pray, and praise, and love.

5 Spirit of light! explore,
And chase our gloom away,
With luster shining more and more,
Unto the perfect day.

234 Come, Holy Spirit, come.

1 COME, Holy Spirit, come,
With energy divine,
And on this poor, benighted soul
With beams of mercy shine.

2 From the celestial hills
Light, life, and joy dispense;
And may I daily, hourly, feel
Thy quickening influence.

3 O melt this frozen heart,
This stubborn will subdue;
Each evil passion overcome,
And form me all anew.

4 The profit will be mine,
But thine shall be the praise;
Cheerful to thee will I devote
The remnant of my days.

235 Come, Holy Spirit.
Tune, Rockingham, opposite page.

1 COME, Holy Spirit, raise our songs
To reach the wonders of that day,
When, with thy fiery, cloven tongues
Thou didst such glorious scenes display.

2 Lord, we believe to us and ours,
The apostolic promise given;
We wait the pentecostal powers,
The Holy Ghost sent down from heaven.

3 Assembled here with one accord,
Calmly we wait the promised grace,
The purchase of our dying Lord;
Come, Holy Ghost, and fill the place.

4 If every one that asks, may find,
If still thou dost on sinners fall,
Come as a mighty, rushing wind;
Great grace be now upon us all.

5 O leave us not to mourn below,
Or long for thy return to pine;
Now, Lord, the Comforter bestow,
And fix in us the Guest divine.

236 O Spirit of the Living God.
Tune, Rockingham, opposite page.

1 O SPIRIT of the living God,
In all thy plenitude of grace,
Where'er the foot of man hath trod,
Descend on our apostate race.

2 Give tongues of fire and hearts of love,
To preach the reconciling word;
Give power and unction from above,
Where'er the joyful sound is heard.

3 Be darkness, at thy coming, light;
Confusion—order, in thy path; [might;
Souls without strength, inspire with
Bid mercy triumph over wrath.

4 Baptize the nations; far and nigh
The triumphs of the cross record;
The name of Jesus glorify,
Till every kindred call him Lord.

INDEX.

	HYMN.		HYMN.		HYMN.
Abide with me,	189	Come on, my partners in	165	Go, labor on; spend and	155
A BLESSING IN PRAYER	91	COME, SPIRIT, COME,	26	Grace! 'tis a charming	195
A bugle note of triumph	134	Come to Jesus, come to	188	Gracious Spirit, love di-	231
Alas! and did my Sav-	170	Come to Jesus, tremb-	53	*Greenville, 8, 7, 4,*	*191*
Alas! how long have I	112	COME, YE BLESSED,	117		
Alida, C. M., d.,	*200*	Come, ye disconsolate,	198	Hail! thou once despised	176
All for Jesus, all for Je-	227	Come, ye sinners, poor	191	HALLELUJAH! AMEN,	39
All is ready, the Master	43	Come, ye that love	206	HAPPY DAY,	224
All my life long I had	144	COMPANIONSHIP WITH	142	HASTE TO THE FIELD	31
ALL THINGS ARE MINE,	94	Consecrate me now, Je-	143	Have you had a kind-	54
Antioch, C. M.,	*212*	CREATION'S HYMN OF	48	Have you something	99
Are you building your	100			HEALING AT THE FOUN	123
Are you happy in the	68	Dark are the waters be-	17	HEAR AND ANSWER	77
Ariel, C. P. M.,	*192*	Dear Saviour, each trial	75	HE CAME TO SAVE ME,	225
A sinner lost, and yet I.	128	*Dennis, S. M.,*	*158*	HE HEARD MY PRAYER	128
As we believe in the gos-	41	Depth of mercy, can	172	Here in the house of the	44
At the cross I've laid	129	Do they know we've	10	HE SAVES ME NOW,	105
AT THE FOUNTAIN,	199	Down at the cross,	181	HE'S MIGHTY TO SAVE,	137
Autumn, 8, 7, d.,	*176*	DOWN, DOWN, DOWN,	101	Holy Ghost, with light	232
Awake, awake, with	138	*Downs, C. M.,*	*152*	Holy, holy, holy, Lord	218
Awake, O Zion's daugh-	4	Draw me, O Lord, with	113	Holy Spirit, Teacher	69
Awake, my soul, stretch	156	DRAW ME TO THEE,	75	HOSANNA!	9
Awake, my soul, to joy-	222			How can we fall if the	116
		Ellesdie, 8, 7, d.,	*178*	How do thy mercies	171
Behold the army of the	13	ENTER NOW,	37	How happy every child	200
BE STILL AND KNOW,	22	Eternal life is in God's	103	HOW LONG?.	63
BEST OF ALL,	18	Eternal beam of light	157	How oft in holy con-	39
BETTER FARTHER ON,	230	*Eventide, 10s,*	*189*	How sweet the name of	152
Beyond the smiling and	210	EVERY KNEE TO HIM	8		
BLESS THE LORD, MY	56			I am praying, blessed	77
Blest are the pure in heart	197	Fade, fade, each earthly	205	I am singing all the day,	19
Blest be the tie that binds	158	Far, far from home, an	55	I am trusting thee, Lord	23
Blow ye the trumpet,	163	*Federal Street, L. M.,*	*171*	I COME TO THEE,	66
Boyleston, S. M.,	*233*	FOLLOWING ON TO KNO	129	I entered once a home	74
		Forest, L. M.,	*182*	If any man thirst,	24
CALLING THEE,	60	For the blessings that we	81	If you want pardon, if	159
Carry me tenderly, Jesus	32	*Fountain, C. M.,*	*219*	I have a song I love to.	79
Children in the temple	9	Fresh springs so holy,	59	I have heard of a land	87
Children of the kingdom	34	FRIENDS, NOT SERVANT	61	I heard the voice of	201
CHRIST IS ALL,	74	From yonder cross what	66	I know not what a day	107
Christmas, C. M.,	*156*	FULL SALVATION,	159	I'LL BE THERE,	180
Come and sit at Jesus'	87			I love thy kingdom, L	194
Come, dear friends, and	106	*Garden,,*	*217*	I LOVE THY WILL,	110
Come, every soul by sin	204	GATHERING HOME,	216	IN THE KINGDOM.	51
Come, Holy S., come,	234	Gently, Lord, O gently	179	In the storm of life,	101
Come, Holy S., heavenly	190	GIVE THANKS,	82	In the way cast up for the	88
Come, Holy S., raise	235	GLORIA PATRI,	211	I thirst, thou wounded	184
Come, let us join our	219	Glory be to the Father,.	211	I TRUST AND WAIT,	107
Come, my soul, thy suit	161	God calling yet! shall I	15	I've found a joy in sor-	145
Come, oh, come to Jesus,	114	God is here and that to	62	I WILL GIVE YOU REST,	14
Come, O Holy Spirit,	26	GOD'S WORD,	89	I will go, I will go, to the	86

THE JOYFUL SOUND.

I will not doubt my Sav-	52	MY ROCK,	40	REVIVE THE HEARTS	62
I will praise the Lord to-	5	My soul for the Saviour	42	REVIVE US AGAIN,	226
I WILL SHOUT HIS PRAIS	98	My soul shouts glory	93	Riches unsearchable,	90
JEHOVAH'S MIGHTY LO	127	Nearer the cross, my heart	185	Salvation, O the joyful	209
Jesus all my grief is shar-	18	NEARER TO THEE,	229	SATISFIED,	144
Jesus calls thee, wand'rer	147	NEVER GO BACK,	116	SAVIOUR, HEAR MY CALL	47
Jesus, I my cross have	178	Nicea, 11, 12, 10,	218	Saviour, lead me, lest I	78
JESUS IS MINE,	205	No other now but Jesus,	38	SAVIOUR, RECEIVE ME,	86
JESUS IS STRONG TO DE-	141	Now to the Lord	174	Scattering the seed, the	115
Jesus is the light, the way	126			Seymour, 7s.,	161
Jesus is waiting his grace	137	O blessed Jesus, O Sav-	1	SHALL WE PRAY FOR	228
JESUS, LOVE ME STILL,	65	O BLESSED WORD,	103	She hath done what she	6
Jesus loves me, fondly	67	O could I speak the	193	Shoulder to shoulder,	133
JESUS, MY JOY,	145	Of him who did salvation	199	SINCE I HAVE BEEN RE-	79
Jesus saves me; blest as-	105	O for a thousand tongues	212	SINGING ALL THE DAY,	19
Jesus, Saviour, comfort.	47	Oft I hear hope sweetly	230	Soldiers for Jesus, rise	36
JESUS SOUGHT ME,	150	O give thanks unto the	82	Soon may the last glad	175
Jesus the meek and lowly	8	O glorious hope of per-	164	Stand up and bless the	196
JESUS, THE SURE FOUN-	100	O happy day that fixed	224	Stand up, stand up for	221
JOY IN HEAVEN,	50	Oh, be joyful in the Lord	104	Stepping-stones to Jesus,	73
Joy to the world,	213	Oh, blessed fellowship	142	Steps are before me, dear	57
Just as thou art, without	168	Oh, how blessed is the	61	St. Martin's, C. M.,	190
		Oh, let us love our broth-	92	SUNSHINE IN THE SOUL,	85
KEEP IN THE LINE,	36	Oh, praise his name for-	102	Sweet land of rest,	203
KINGDOM, POWER, AND	111	Oh, rally round the stand-	12		
		Oh, the deep, unfathomed	127	TAKE ALL MY SINS AWA	160
Land ahead! a light is	130	Oh, the Lord is rich in	124	Take the hand thy Sav-	35
Land of bliss, where the	11	Oh, the time is flying fast	51	TELL IT OUT WITH	68
Lead me, lead me, lead.	95	Oh, wake, for the day is	31	THE ARMY OF THE L.	13
LEAD ME, SAVIOUR,	78	Oh, we are young soldiers	136	THE BANNER OF THE	30
LEARN OF HIM,	87	Oh, what utter weakness	65	THE BEAUTIFUL LIGHT	126
LET BROTHERLY LOVE	92	Oh, why do you linger	84	The Bible was given,	89
LET ME INTO NOTHING	21	Oh, why should we wres-	146	The Christ is found,	167
LET US NOT BE WEARY,	115	Oh, why thus stand with	27	THE CONQUEROR,	29
Lischer, H. M.,	163	O love divine, how sweet	192	The gospel word, so freely	7
Listen to the "still, small	16	ONE IN THEE,	46	The heavenly Father calls	60
Little sunbeams in their	96	ONLY BELIEVE,	146	THE HEAVENWARD WA	28
Long, weary years in sin	150	ONLY TRUST HIM,	204	THE HOUSE OF THE L.	44
Looking to Jesus, bright	131	O North, with all thy	29	The Lord into his gar-	217
Lord God, the Holy G.	233	OPEN THOU MINE EYES,	122	THE LORD IS GOOD,	70
Lord, I am thine, entire-	183	Open your heart to Jesus	125	THE LORD IS RICH IN	124
Lord, with all my heart,	49	Oppressed by countless	14	The Lord's my shepherd	154
LOOK AND BELIEVE,	167	O SAVIOUR, STAY,	112	THE MORNING DRAW-	12
Lo! round the throne	173	O sing of the power of	108	The morning light is	220
Louvan, L. M.,	157	O Spirit of the living G.	236	The past we never can	80
Love divine, all love	177	O spotless Lamb, I come	160	THE PLEADING SAV-	147
Loving-kindness, L. M.,	222	O that my load of sin	182	THE PRECIOUS LOVE OF	108
Luther, S. M.,	194	Our fatherland, thy name	58	There is a fountain filled	169
		Our Sunday-school, how	120	There is a land of pure	180
Maitland, C. M.,	162	Outside the gate, and yet	37	There is healing at the	123
Manoah, C. M.,	151	OVER THE TIDE,	17	There is joy among the	50
MARCHING IN THE	88			There is perfect cleansing	148
MARCHING ON TO VIC-	132	Park Street, L. M.,	173	There is rest, sweet rest,	91
Missionary Chant, L. M.,	155	PASS IT ON,	54	THERE'S A BLESSING	148
More about Jesus would	109	Pleyel's Hymn, 7s.,	172, 231	There's a great day com-	118
MORE LIKE JESUS,	57	Praise God on the throne	48	There's a hand held out	72
Mourn for the thousands	214	Praise him for his glory,	56	There's a mansion for me	25
Must Jesus bear the cross	162	PRAISE HIM, OH, PRAISE	1	There's a place for me	64
My faith, inspired with	46	Praise the Lord for his	25	There's sunshine in my	85
My faith looks up to thee,	223	Praise the Lord, ye heav-	121	THE SAVING GRACE OF	41
MY HEART'S DEAR	149			THE STILL, SMALL VOIC	16
MY JESUS STILL SAVES	71	Return, O ye lost ones,	119	The temperance cause is	132

INDEX.

The world was like a	71	VICTORY IS NEAR,	134	When Jesus laid his	225
THE WORDS OF THIS	7			When life is full of toil	22
Thou art a Rock in a	40	Waiting by the wayside,	122	When lost among the	149
Thy will to me, O Lord,	110	*Watchman, 7s, d.,*	153	When our Saviour in his	117
Till he come, oh, let	186	Watchman, tell us of the	153	When we come with bur-	228
'Tis mine to walk in the	94	We are going forth to	30	WHY LINGER?	84
To-day the Redeemer is	63	*Webb, 7.6,*	220	*Willoughby, C. P. M.,*	164
To-day the Saviour calls	187	Welcome, delightful	166	WILL YOU COME TO JE-	27
To Father, Son, and H.	209	We praise thee, O God,	226	With trembling contri-	28
To God the Father,	197	We praise thee, our Fa-	111	Wonderful, Lord, thy	20
To us a child of hope is	208	We shall walk the realms	33	Work, for the night is	202
TRUSTING ON,	49	What glory gilds the	207	Work, oh, work for Jesus	83
TRUSTING ONLY THEE,	23	What ruin hath intemp-	215	Worthy to be praised is	45
Trust not the path before	97	WHAT THE LORD HAS	106		
TURN UNTO ME,	97	WHAT WILL THE FIRST	76	You ask what makes me	98
		When all thy mercies, O	151	YOUNG SOLDIERS FOR J.	136
Unfold in beauty, flower	70	When doubt and conflict	229		
Up to the bountiful Giver	216	Whene'er I think of Je-	21	*Zerah, C. M.,*	206
		When in the tempest he'll	141		

www.ingramcontent.com/pod-product-compliance
Lightning Source LLC
Chambersburg PA
CBHW032137160426
43197CB00008B/675